Creative Ideas
with
Hardanger

Creative Ideas
with
Hardanger

DOROTHY WOOD

Photographs by Shona Wood

NEW
HOLLAND

To Mum – I guess it must be in the genes

First published in 2001 by
New Holland Publishers (UK) Ltd
London • Cape Town • Sydney • Auckland

Garfield House
86 Edgware Road
London W2 2EA
United Kingdom

80 McKenzie Street
Cape Town 8001
South Africa

Level 1, Unit 4, 14 Aquatic Drive
Frenchs Forest, NSW 2086
Australia

218 Lake Road
Northcote, Auckland
New Zealand

1 3 5 7 9 10 8 6 4 2

ISBN 1 85974 449 4

Editor: Gillian Haslam
Design: Roger Daniels
Photography: Shona Wood
Production: Caroline Hansell
Editorial Direction: Rosemary Wilkinson

Reproduction by Modern Age Repro House Ltd, Hong Kong
Printed and bound in Malaysia by Times Offset (M) Sdn. Bhd.

Acknowledgements:
The author would like to thank Cara Ackerman at DMC Creative World
for supplying the DMC threads and Zweigart fabric used for the projects.

Special thanks go to Jenny Blair, Isabel Hamilton, Michaela Learner, Rosemary Munden,
Brenda Sandford-Monk and Adelle Wainwright for their help in stitching the projects.

Contents

In the
LIVING ROOM

In the
DINING ROOM

In the
BEDROOM

Introduction

I first became interested in Hardanger a few years ago when I admired a table centre stitched by my aunt. I have always enjoyed drawn thread work, having used the technique when embroidering my wedding dress and the family christening robe, and was therefore keen to try Hardanger. I have to say I was immediately hooked! It is a technique that is relaxing to work and it is fascinating to watch the design develop as you stitch. Hardanger relies on the beauty of the stitches rather than clever combinations of colours and threads, and so can be enjoyed by those of us who are not too artistic. The designs are generally based on geometric motifs worked individually or repeated across the fabric and the basic stitches are so easy to learn that they can be perfected with the minimum of practice.

Hardanger embroidery is an ancient form of peasant embroidery combining counted thread work with delicate needle weaving and needle lace. Experts believe its origins can be traced back to Persia where coloured silk threads were stitched on delicate cotton gauze. From there, the technique spread to Europe and became very popular in Italy, where the technique of cut and pulled threads was developed to create beautiful cutwork embroidery combined with exquisite lace edgings. The modern style of this attractive embroidery technique comes from the area surrounding the beautiful Hardanger fjord on the west coast of Norway, where it was introduced from Italy in the seventeenth century. The

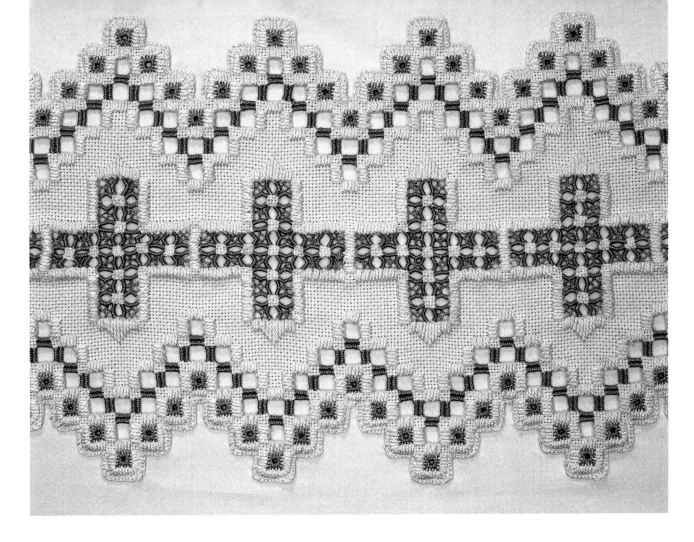

oldest known piece of Hardanger from the region is an apron
stitched by Gunbjørg Midtbø at the beginning of the eighteenth
century, which uses similar techniques and design to Italian
embroidery from the late seventeenth century.

Hardanger embroidery was traditionally stitched using linen
threads on fine linen fabrics with counts of between 25 and 50
threads per inch. The linen was produced locally from home-
grown flax and was originally used to decorate skirts and aprons.
The lace work on these garments was so beautiful that they were
worn for celebrations and weddings and were so prevalent that
they eventually became part of the traditional costume of the
area. As Hardanger embroidery grew in popularity, it was used
to decorate a range of soft furnishings, such as table linen, bed
linen, cushions and curtains. The embroidery technique, now

known simply as Hardanger, has been further developed over the years by women in the Hardanger region of Norway and is renowned throughout the world.

In keeping with the tradition of making beautiful things for the home, for this book I have designed a wide selection of beautiful projects that can be made to keep for yourself, or to give as gifts. There are three chapters, each connected with a different room in the house – the living room, bedroom and dining room. In the living room there is a practical fire screen, an unusual scatter cushion, beautiful tie backs, an eye-catching blind, and a pair of heart-shaped window hangings. In the dining room you will find a selection of table linen – a beautiful tablecloth which can be altered in size to suit your own table, a gorgeous table centre, a stunning table runner, colourful napkins and an unusual tablemat and coaster that will look equally stunning in classic white or a colour to suit your furnishings. The bedroom has a tablemat and matching trinket pot for the dressing table, an exquisite lavender sachet, an attractive duvet cover, a delicate pure linen pillowcase and a pretty shelf border. The projects vary in skill level, so beginners and more experienced stitchers alike will find something here to suit their level of ability. Some projects, such as the fire screen on page 41, are quite large and time-consuming but not at all technically difficult. Others, such as the lavender sachet on page 76, require a greater degree of expertise.

This book provides clear and precise instructions that will allow even the novice stitcher to complete a design with confidence. I have been told that what holds most people back from trying this technique is the difficulty associated with cutwork – many worry that the work will disintegrate if they cut

the wrong threads. In reality, because the work progresses in a strict and logical order, it is difficult to make a mistake and if by chance the wrong thread is cut, it is quite easy to weave in a replacement. Hardanger is a technique that embroiderers who enjoy other counted thread techniques should try as it can complement and add interest to cross stitch or black work designs. The beauty of Hardanger is the freedom to choose your own thread colours and fabric. Each of the projects in the book could have been stitched white on white and the charts would have been exactly the same. Once inspired by the beautiful photographs, you can choose to stitch the designs in colours to match the décor in your own home.

If you have not stitched Hardanger before, first work through the technique section to learn the basic stitches and how to cut the threads on a small sample of fabric before beginning on a larger piece. Hardanger is a beautiful and incredibly addictive embroidery technique, which will give you many hours of pleasure for years to come.

Techniques

Hardanger is based on groups of satin stitches called kloster blocks that are arranged diagonally or in straight lines across the fabric. Threads are cut within these blocks and removed to leave straight threads that can be woven or wrapped and decorated with filling stitches. The fabric around the cutwork is often embellished with other types of embroidery such as satin stitch motifs, eyelets and backstitch. Hardanger is worked in a strict sequence and all kloster blocks and surface embroidery must be stitched before you cut the threads. It is advisable to practise the stitches and cutting on a piece of spare fabric before beginning your chosen project.

Fabrics for Hardanger

Hardanger is a counted thread embroidery technique that is worked on an evenweave fabric. An evenweave fabric has the same number of threads running horizontally and vertically.

There are many different evenweave fabrics suitable for Hardanger, from fine Belfast linen to the coarse Davosa. Other popular fabrics used for this type of embroidery include Linda, Lugana, Bellana and Hardanger. Some fabrics are 100 per cent linen or a cotton/linen mix, while others are pure cotton or a cotton and rayon mix. Most fabrics are available in a wide range of colours, although some, such as Damask Hardanger, are only available in white or cream.

The fabrics are interchangeable in the majority of the projects but take care to choose one with similar properties. Fabrics can appear to be similar but may not be suitable. For example, Dublin linen has a loose weave that is not suitable for buttonhole edging, whereas Belfast linen has a much denser weave and can have a buttonhole edge. Damask Hardanger drapes beautifully and is therefore ideal for tablecloths, but standard Hardanger is much firmer and only suitable for flat projects such as mats.

Each of the charts provided in this book can be used for different counts of fabric but the motif size will change if the count size is different. As the charts have two threads to each block of the chart, double the number of blocks the design is worked over and then divide by the count of the fabric to find the finished size.

For example, if the chart is 64 blocks square:

On Belfast linen (32 count) the design will be 10 cm (4 in) square.
$64 \times 2 = 128$; divide this by 32 = 4 inches. Multiply by 2.5 to find the size in centimetres.

On Lugana (25 count) the design will be 13 cm (5 in) square.
$64 \times 2 = 128$; divide this by 25 = 5.1 inches. Multiply by 2.5 to find the size in centimetres.

On Davosa (18 count) the design will be 18 cm (7 in) square.
$64 \times 2 = 128$; divide this by 18 = 7.1 inches. Multiply by 2.5 to find the size in centimetres.

The Zweigart fabrics used in this book are as follows:

Hardanger – 22 count
This is a 100 per cent cotton fabric, available in a wide range of colours, 110 cm (43 in) wide. Hardanger is very easy to stitch and cut. It does not drape very well and is better for flat linen, such as tablemats.

Damask Hardanger – 22 count

This is a 55 per cent cotton/45 per cent viscose fabric, available in cream and white only, 170 cm (67 in) wide. Damask Hardanger is a unique fabric that makes absolutely beautiful table centres or tablecloths. It is not for the novice as the threads are difficult to count.

Belfast linen – 32 count

This is a 100 per cent linen fabric, available in a wide range of colours, 140 cm (55 in) wide. Belfast linen is traditional, closely woven linen. It requires experience to stitch but the results are exceptional. A magnifying lamp will allow greater accuracy.

Dublin linen – 25 count

This is a 100 per cent linen fabric, available in a small range of colours, 140 cm (55 in) wide. Dublin linen is woven from finely spun threads slightly spaced to give a translucent effect. It is not suitable for buttonhole edges.

Linda – 27 count

This is a 100 per cent cotton fabric, available in an extensive range of colours, both 85 cm (33 in) and 140 cm (55 in) wide. Linda is a fairly fine fabric that handles like pure linen but is less expensive.

Lugana – 25 count

This is a 52 per cent cotton/48 per cent viscose fabric, available in a wide range of colours, 140 cm (55 in) wide. Lugana is beautiful fabric for Hardanger as it drapes beautifully. Although the stitches are quite small, the fabric is easy to stitch. It is an excellent choice for table linen.

Bellana – 20 count

This is a 52 per cent cotton/48 per cent viscose fabric, available in a small range of colours, 140 cm (55 in) wide. The viscose content gives this fabric a slight sheen and soft handle. It is quick to stitch on and the finished Hardanger has a more delicate appearance than Davosa.

Davosa – 18 count

This is a 100 per cent cotton fabric, available in a small range of colours, 140 cm (55 in) wide. It has a loose, even weave that is ideal for beginners to work with. The work progresses quickly because of the ease of stitching and the larger scale.

Threads for Hardanger

Hardanger embroidery looks much better stitched with a round thread, such as coton perlé. This type of thread allows the stitches to be quite distinct and to stand out from the fabric. Two different thicknesses of thread are used for each piece of Hardanger. The kloster blocks and other satin stitch embroidery are stitched in a thread that is slightly thicker than the fabric threads. The needle weaving, lace and eyelets are stitched in a finer thread. The thickness of the thread therefore depends on the count of fabric. Coton perlé is available in sizes 3, 5, 8 and 12.

Check the project instructions to find the thread thickness required for each fabric, or refer to the chart below.

Fabric	Count	Needle size	Thread size
Hardanger	22	22 and 24	No. 5 and no. 8
Damask Hardanger	22	22 and 24	No. 5 and no. 8
Belfast linen	32	24 and 26	No. 8 and no. 12
Dublin linen	25	24 and 26	No. 5 and no. 8
Linda	27	24 and 26	No. 5 and no. 8
Lugana	25	24 and 26	No. 5 and no. 8
Bellana	20	22 and 24	No. 5 and no. 8
Davosa	18	20 and 22	No. 3 and no. 5

Getting Started

If you have not stitched Hardanger before, I recommend that you read through this techniques chapter, actually stitching the examples as you go so that you learn exactly how to create the stitches. Although it looks straightforward, if the stitch sequence is not followed, threads may go across areas that will be cut at a later stage. Choose a fabric such as 25 count Lugana or 20 count Bellana which have a smooth surface and are not too fine (see the previous pages for more information on fabrics).

Use no. 5 coton perlé for the kloster blocks, satin stitch embroidery and any buttonhole edging. The finer no. 8 coton perlé is used for the weaving, wrapping, needle lace, eyelets and backstitch. A size 24 tapestry needle is ideal for the no. 5 coton perlé and a finer size 26 needle for the no. 8 perlé.

The following tips are useful for both beginners and more experienced stitchers

- Work Hardanger from the right side, holding the fabric in the hand rather than using a hoop.

- Never use knots to secure the embroidery thread. To begin, leave an 8 cm (3 in) tail secured by a couple of backstitches. These can be unpicked and woven in under some stitches on the reverse side later.

- For accuracy and to avoid eyestrain, use a magnifying lamp for both stitching and cutting. Always work in good light.

- Remember that charts have two threads to each small square. Enlarge the charts by photocopying if necessary.

- Work methodically, checking stitches and blocks line up.

- Complete all surface stitching and double check that the blocks are accurately aligned before you begin to cut threads.

- Work the same number of stitches on each wrapped or woven bar, but take care as the embroidery will be distorted if you try to fit too many stitches in each.

- Work diagonally rather than in straight lines when stitching from one bar to the next.

- If you are inserting a web after completing the bars, use a fine embroidery needle, rather than a blunt-ended tapestry needle.

Hardanger Stitches

There is a wide variety of stitches used in Hardanger embroidery, and all of them are simple to learn and execute. The intricacy of this embroidery comes from the combination of the different stitches used to create an infinite number of designs.

KLOSTER BLOCKS

Kloster blocks are groups of five satin stitches worked over four threads of linen, worked diagonally or in a straight line. The blocks appear in a geometric shape, usually a diamond or square. The two techniques can be combined to make more ornate shapes.

WORKING IN A STRAIGHT LINE

Kloster blocks are worked in a straight line to make square and rectangular motifs. If the threads are counted correctly, the last block will touch the first.

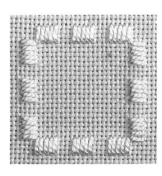

1 Begin by working two small backstitches, leaving a tail of thread that will be sewn in later. Work five satin stitches over four threads of linen.

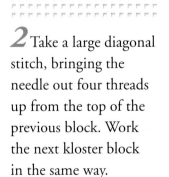

2 Take a large diagonal stitch, bringing the needle out four threads up from the top of the previous block. Work the next kloster block in the same way.

3 To turn a corner, on the last stitch turn the needle at right angles and bring it out four threads away. Work the next block.

4 Continue working around the sides in the same way, working three kloster blocks on each side of the square until you end up back where you started.

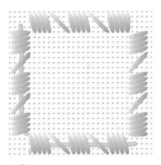

5 Slip the needle under two blocks of stitches on the reverse side and trim the thread. Unpick the backstitches and sew the ends in on the reverse.

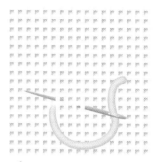

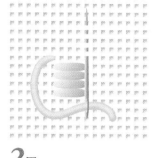

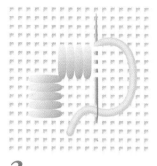

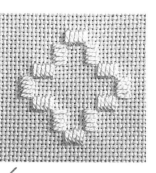

1 Begin by working two small backstitches, leaving a tail of thread that will be sewn in later. Work five satin stitches over four threads of linen.

2 To turn a corner, on the last stitch, turn the needle at right angles and bring it out four threads away. Work the next block.

3 On the next corner, take a backstitch to bring the needle out at the opposite end of the last stitch. Work the next block at right angles to the first.

4 Work four kloster blocks on each side of the diamond, changing the stitch angle by alternating steps 2 and 3, until you end up where you started.

CUTTING THE THREADS

The threads are not cut until all the kloster blocks and surface embroidery have been completed. Check that the blocks are exactly opposite one another and that no threads have been skipped. If you have arrived back where you started, the stitching is likely to be accurate. Use fine pointed scissors to cut the threads.

CUTTING THREADS ON LARGER MOTIFS

Check that the stitches are worked along a thread and count each side carefully before cutting. Cut the threads in groups of four rather than trying to cut across eight or twelve threads at once.

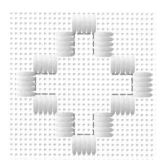

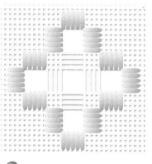

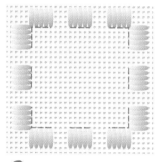

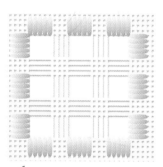

1 Only cut threads between satin stitches and not at the end of a block. There are five satin stitches with four fabric threads in-between to cut.

2 Pull the cut threads out with tweezers to leave a grid of threads arranged in a square pattern. On a square block the remaining threads form a cross.

3 On larger motifs, follow the cut threads across and cut the other end on the opposite side of the motif.

4 Work around the motif, cutting the remaining threads. Pull the cut threads out to leave a grid of threads, as shown.

Needle Weaving and Needle Lace

Needle weaving and needle lace are worked over the thread bars left once the cutwork is complete. Wrapping or weaving the thread bars has a dual purpose. It not only adds decorative embroidery, but also strengthens the fabric as the stitches are so firmly packed. This solid embroidery can be given a more delicate appearance with the addition of needle lace stitches.

WRAPPED BARS

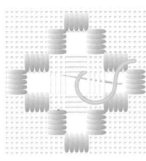 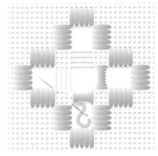 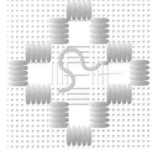

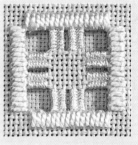

1 Secure the thread on the reverse side by slipping the needle under two or three kloster blocks. Keep your finger behind the fabric threads to tension them slightly and overcast the fabric threads quite tightly.

2 Take the needle across the back to wrap the next bar. Work around the block and secure the thread on the reverse side.

VARIATION
DOUBLE BARS
Groups of eight threads can also be worked as double woven bars.

WOVEN BARS

 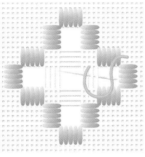 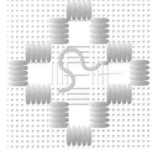 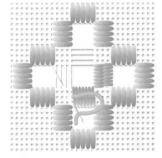

1 Secure the perlé thread on the reverse side by slipping the needle under two or three kloster blocks. Bring the needle out in the middle of the group of fabric threads and take a backstitch over the first two threads.

2 Weave over and under two threads, pulling the thread quite tight for each stitch. Continue weaving in a figure of eight pattern until the bar is full. The stitches should be tight and even.

3 Take the needle to the reverse side and bring it out in the middle of the next group of threads to be woven. Continue until all the bars are woven and sew the ends in on the reverse side.

WOVEN BARS WITH PICOTS

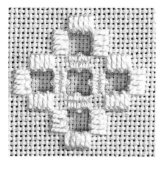

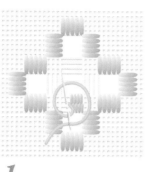

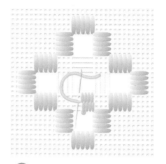

Woven bars with picots are one of the prettiest stitches in Hardanger. The picot can be worked on one side only, or both as shown here.

1 Weave half the way across the fabric threads and insert the needle half way into the bar. Wrap the thread around the needle and pull the needle through to form the picot.

2 Weave the needle through in the opposite direction and make a picot stitch on the other side. Complete the woven bar. For a larger picot knot, a chain stitch can be worked into the picot.

DOVE'S EYE FILLING

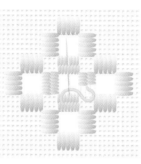

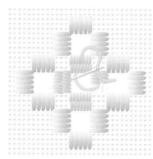

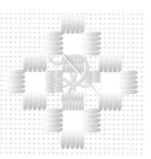

Also known as a web, this is one of the most common lace stitches. It can be worked on both woven and wrapped bars.

1 Weave or wrap three of the bars. On the last one, work halfway across the fabric threads then take a small stitch through the centre of the next bar.

2 Take the needle under the first part of the web, bringing the needle out in the middle of the next bar.

3 Take a stitch into each bar in turn until you are back where you started. Complete the weaving or wrapping on the last bar.

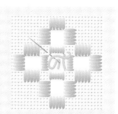

VARIATION

LACE STITCH This is a similar stitch to Dove's eye filling, worked into the corners of the square.

OPEN CENTRE SQUARES

Larger cutwork motifs are worked with decorative satin stitch borders rather than the basic kloster block. The larger cutwork areas are filled with ornate needlelace designs.

The satin stitches can vary in length to create a variety of patterns. There have to be a certain number of stitches, so that the threads can be grouped and cut in the same way as the smaller

kloster blocks. As there is a fabric thread between each satin stitch, work one more satin stitch than the threads required on each side.

The samples shown below are all based on a 12-thread square with 13 satin stitches on each side. Larger cutwork squares are based on the four times table, as the threads are cut or woven in groups or multiples of four.

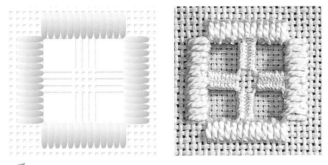

1 Straight edge

Work one more satin stitch than the threads required on each side of the square. Cut the first four threads and the last four on each side of the square. Wrap or weave the bars.

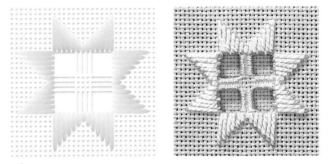

3 Star edge

Work the first satin stitch over eight threads and then work over one less thread each stitch until the centre stitch is over two threads. Work back up stitching over eight threads to complete the side.

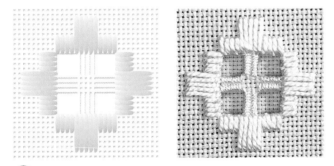

2 Crenellated edge

Work four satin stitches over four threads, and then five stitches over eight threads, then complete the side with four stitches over four threads again. Cut the threads in the same way as the straight edge.

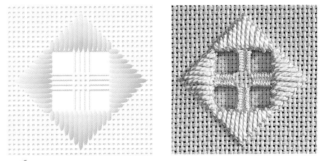

4 Diamond edge

Work the first satin stitch over two threads and then work over one more thread each stitch until the centre stitch is over eight threads. Work back down stitching over two threads to complete the side.

Needle Lace Filling Stitches

DARNING INSERTION STITCH

Darning insertion stitch is an ornate stitch that is worked in several stages to fill large cutwork squares.

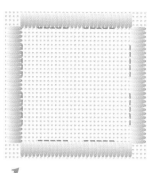

1 This stitch is worked in a square with 29 satin stitches on each side. Leave four threads at each end and cut eight threads on either side of the four centre threads.

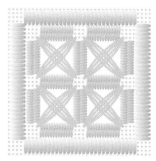

2 Weave the thread bars around the outside and then carry four threads diagonally across each square in both directions. Weave these thread bars.

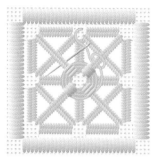

3 Work a woven wheel in the centre of the large square using the same weight of thread as the satin stitch. Begin in the centre and work outwards, over-sewing each of the spokes of the wheel to form the distinctive ridges.

ADJOINING WRAP

This is an attractive filling stitch which creates a small windmill shape in the centre of the square.

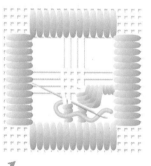

1 This stitch is worked in a square with 13 satin stitches on each side. Cut four threads at each end leaving four in the centre. Wrap two threads together.

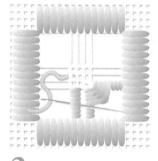

2 Bring the needle out in the middle of the next group of threads and then work back out, weaving across in a figure of eight to form a triangle shape. Wrap the remaining threads together. Continue in the same way until complete.

Leaf shape

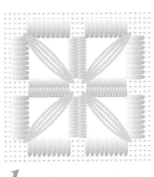

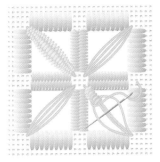

This is a less well known filling stitch that was commonly used in traditional Hardanger. It can be worked in a woven trellis or as a filling in open squares.

1 Work a square with nine satin stitches either side of the centre four fabric threads. Cut the threads to prepare the open square. Weave the bars, then carry a double thread diagonally across the square in both directions. Work a slightly looser single thread on either side.

2 Weave under and over the diagonal threads to form a leaf shape. The outside threads can be held in shape with pins or tacking thread or simply support the threads with your finger.

Shuttle stitch

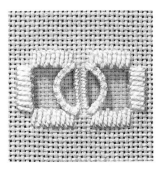

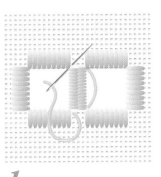

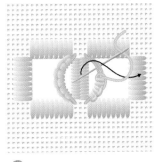

Shuttle stitch is a form of buttonhole bars that is worked in a semi-circle across an open square.

1 Work two small open squares with nine satin stitches, side by side with a woven bar in the centre. Stitch a long double thread on either side of the woven bar.

2 To work shuttle stitch along the bars. Make an ordinary buttonhole stitch and then take the needle under the thread bar and back out under the working thread.

Surface Embroidery Stitches

There is a seemingly endless variation of embroidery possible in Hardanger and some of the surface stitches are found in other forms of counted thread embroidery such canvas work, needlepoint, pulled thread and drawn thread work. The most common stitch, that gives Hardanger much of its character, is satin stitch. This is worked horizontally, vertically and diagonally to create beautiful motifs. The other popular stitches are eyelets, worked inside a small square of kloster blocks, backstitch and cable stitch, a stitch used in pulled thread work.

SATIN STITCH

Satin stitch can be used to produce a wide range of different geometric and naturalistic motifs to fill in the fabric areas around the cutwork. The number of motifs is limitless but some, such as the tulip and eight-pointed star, are very popular. Use the same thickness of thread as for the kloster blocks.

TULIP

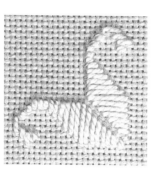

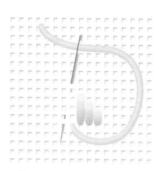

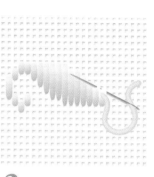

1 Count the threads carefully, work the satin stitches for the first side of the tulip.

2 Work the second side of the tulip, using the same holes for the threads in the centre of the tulip.

EIGHT-POINTED STAR

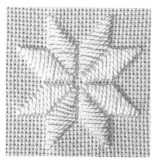

1 Count the threads carefully, working the number of stitches indicated on your chart.

2 Continue around the star, using the same holes for the threads that butt together.

BACKSTITCH

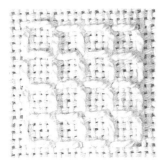 

Backstitch is used for small areas of straight stitches, especially where areas are filled with grids for texture.

Begin with a backstitch over two or four threads and then bring the needle out the same number of threads in front of the first stitch. Work each subsequent stitch in the same way.

HOLBEIN STITCH

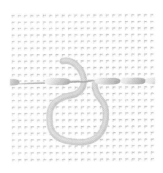

Holbein stitch is sometimes called double running stitch and looks similar to backstitch. It has a more even appearance than backstitch and is more suitable for long lines of surface embroidery.

Work a line of running stitches, leaving the same sized space between each stitch. Go back and fill in the gaps, inserting the needle above the stitch and bringing the thread out below the next.

CABLE STITCH

Cable stitch can be pulled slightly to draw the threads, forming tiny holes or simply stitched as a diagonal backstitch. Use a finer thread for pulled work on loose weave linens and heavier thread for a bold line.

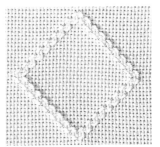

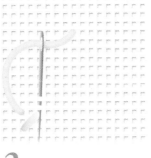 

1 Take a stitch diagonally over two threads and then bring the needle out two threads to one side.

2 Make another stitch diagonally and bring out at the top of the first stitch.

3 Continue working diagonally alternating the needle from row to row to create two parallel lines of stitches.

4 To turn the corner, turn the needle in the corner hole to make a stitch at right angles and then continue as before.

EYELETS

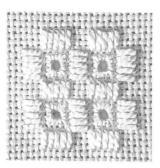

Eyelets can be worked in a range of different sizes, but are usually worked in the centre of a small square of kloster blocks, using the finer thread.

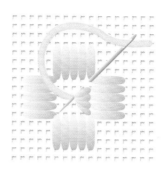

Work into the same hole as each satin stitch all the way round the square. Pull the threads firmly to form a hole in the centre.

Finishing the Edges of the Embroidery

There are several alternatives that can be used to finish the edges of Hardanger. The one you choose will depend on the type of fabric, the finished appearance required, how the item will be used and how often it is likely to be laundered. Buttonhole stitch is the traditional way to finish Hardanger embroidery. It can only be used on fairly firm, close woven fabric and creates an intricate, decorative edge on table linen, blinds and shelf borders. For a stronger hem that can be laundered regularly, choose one of the straight edge hems finished by hand or machine stitching.

BUTTONHOLE STITCH

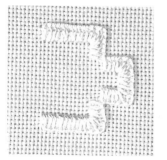

Buttonhole stitch is worked on the linen before the cutwork is started and can form part of the kloster block design. Once complete, cut the fabric away, taking care not to cut any embroidery threads.

1 Work the buttonhole stitch over four threads. Use simple buttonhole stitch rather than the knotted buttonhole stitch used in tailoring.

2 At the corner use the same centre hole and then insert the needle into every second hole for the next four stitches.

3 Stitch next edge. To turn an inward corner, use the last stitch hole for the first stitch on the second side.

Hems

Pieces of Hardanger that will be laundered regularly, such as table linen, can be finished with a double hem. There are several different ways to finish a double hem, some practical and others more decorative.

NARROW MACHINE-STITCHED

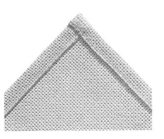

This hem is commonly used on the edge of napkins and tablecloths. Trim the linen along a thread, 1 cm (½ in) larger than required. Press under 5 mm (¼ in) on all sides, then trim the corners along the folds. Turn under the two sides to make a 5 mm (¼ in) double hem and machine-stitch. Turn under the top and bottom edges and machine-stitch to complete the hem.

MITRING A CORNER

This is the neatest way to finish hems wider than 1 cm (½ in). Tack the finished size of the linen. Measure out twice the depth of the finished hem and trim the linen along a thread.

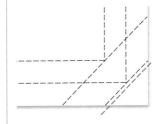

1 Fold the raw edge into the tacked line, then fold again; press. Open out the hem. Fold the corner diagonally across the first pressed line. Trim 5 mm (¼ in) away from the fold.

2 Re-fold and slipstitch across the mitre. The inside edge of the hem can be stitched by machine or hemstitched.

HEMSTITCH

Often used on table linen, hemstitch can be worked on one side only, catching in the hem as you stitch or worked as a deeper border on both sides. Threads are cut and drawn out on the inside edge of the hem, then stitched in groups to form a series of holes.

1 Mitre the hem and tack. Snip across two threads in the centre of one side of the hem, level with the inside fold. Pull the fabric threads out in each direction until you reach the corner. Snip and pull threads on each side in the same way.

2 Trim the fabric threads to 1 cm (½ in) and tuck under the hem at each corner. Work hemstitch from the right side, gathering the threads into equal sized bundles of 2-4 threads and catching the hem on the reverse side as you go.

VARIATION
To make a deeper hemstitch border, cut and draw out more threads, say ten or twelve, and work hemstitch along the other edge. The threads can be grouped to form bars or a zigzag pattern.

With so many varied soft furnishings, the living room is the ideal place to display your Hardanger embroidery. Choose from three ideas to enhance windows – a charming lacy blind, classic curtain tiebacks or delicate, heart-shaped window hangings. Alternatively, make a stunning fire screen to cover an empty grate or stitch a beautiful panelled cushion for the armchair or sofa.

in the LIVING ROOM

Scatter Cushion

Whether tucked into the corner of a wicker chair or arranged along a sofa, cushions not only add extra comfort but can also introduce a contrasting colour or texture to the living room. This scatter cushion has an unusual openwork panel of Hardanger set between panels of dark grey peach-skin fabric. The large square stitches are known as darning insertion stitch and can be worked as a square panel in the centre of a cushion or, as 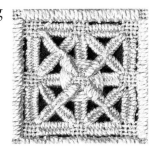 shown here, in a long strip down the centre of a rectangular cushion. Use a colour of thread that matches the colour of the fabric to enhance the beauty of the cutwork and back with a darker fabric so the cutwork stands out.

Working the Hardanger

1 Cut a 40 × 20 cm (16 × 8 in) piece of Lugana fabric. Zigzag around the edge to prevent the fabric fraying while stitching. Tack a box 30 × 10.5 cm (12 × 4¼ in) centrally on the evenweave fabric.

2 Starting in one corner of the tacked box, stitch the kloster block grid first using no. 5 coton perlé. Here, there are 29 stitches over four threads on each side of the squares.

3 To cut the threads on each side of the square, leave the first four threads and cut the next eight. Then leave the middle four and

cut the next eight. Carefully pull the cut threads out once you have cut all four sides in the same way.

4 Using no. 8 coton perlé, work woven thread bars across the remaining fabric threads.

5 Beginning in one corner, take a thread diagonally across the large square, stitching into the centre woven square as you go. Go back across on the under side, catching the thread in the centre. Repeat again so that there are two threads above and another two below. Stitch four threads across between the other two corners.

6 Work four threads across each of the small squares in the same way to complete the grid. Weave thread bars on all the diagonal threads.

7 To complete the stitch, use no. 5 perlé to work a ribbed wheel in the centre. This is a variation of the darning insertion stitch. Work a backstitch over each of the diagonal threads four times to create a solid circle of stitches.

Making up

8 Neatly trim the Hardanger panel all round, leaving a 1.5 cm (⅝ in) seam allowance. Zigzag the seams on the machine to prevent the fabric fraying.

9 Cut two 15 × 31 cm (6 × 12¼ in) panels in grey fabric. Pin the panels down each side of the Hardanger panel and tack. Machine-stitch from the reverse side, exactly along the outside edge of the kloster blocks.

10 Press the seams away from the Hardanger. Cut a 31 × 40 cm (12¼ × 16 in) panel of grey fabric. Tack to the reverse side of the front of the cushion cover.

11 Cut two 31 cm (12¼ in) square panels in grey fabric. Turn under and press a double 2 cm (¾ in) hem along one edge of each. Machine-stitch along the inner fold.

12 Place the front cushion panel face up. With right sides together, pin one panel to each end. Overlap the panels and pin the side seams. Machine-stitch around the edge, reverse stitching across the overlap for strength. Trim across the corners and turn through. Insert the cushion pad through the envelope opening.

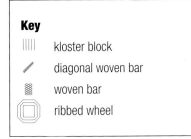

Key

‖‖	kloster block
⁄	diagonal woven bar
▓	woven bar
⬡	ribbed wheel

Curtain Tiebacks

Tiebacks are the ideal solution to prevent curtains from blowing about when a window is left open. They also hold the curtain back from the window, allowing the maximum amount of daylight to enter the room. Depending on the thread and fabric chosen, you can change the look of the tieback to suit different curtain fabrics. For sheer or lightweight curtains, use the loosely woven Dublin linen to create a delicate tieback. On more substantial curtains, use a firmer fabric such as Linda.

The length of the tieback will depend on 'the embrace'. This is the measurement around the curtain from the tieback hook. Hold a tape measure at the height you want the tieback and take it around the curtain so it holds the fabric without crushing it. Blouse the curtain out over the top and measure. Add 2.5 cm (1 in) at each end of the stitching for the finished length. There is no need to work Hardanger all the way across what will be the back – one pattern repeat beyond the centre line will suffice.

YOU WILL NEED:

Evenweave fabric: Dublin linen in white or Linda in light blue 510
DMC perlé: white or blue 932 nos. 5 and 8 coton perlé
Four small curtain rings
Sewing kit
Coton perlé no. 8 (for making up)

Finished size of stitching:

Depth of border: approximately 8 cm (3 in)
Width of one repeat: Dublin Linen 7 cm (2¾ in)
Linda 6.5 cm (2⅝ in)

Finished length of tieback:

Approximately 56 cm (22 in) for five diamonds; approximately 64 cm (25 in) for six diamonds

Working the Hardanger

1 Work out the length of the tieback as explained on page 32 and cut a piece of fabric at least 8 cm (3 in) larger all round for each tieback. Fold the fabric in half crossways. Using no. 5 perlé, work the kloster blocks for the figure of eight motif in the centre. Stitch the required number of repeats across a piece of evenweave, remembering that there is no need for you to embroider beyond one repeat on one side (this will form the back of the tieback and will be hidden behind the curtain).

2 Refer to the chart and work eyelets in the groups of kloster blocks along each edge, using no. 5 perlé.

3 Cut the threads across the end of the kloster blocks in each of the diamond and figure of eight motifs. If you are unsure which threads to cut, refer to the techniques section on page 16. Pull the cut threads out.

4 Using no. 8 perlé, work wrapped bars in the figure of eight motifs and woven bars in the diamonds, working Dove's eye filling in four of the cut squares as shown.

5 As the design is reversible, stitch a second tieback in exactly the same way.

Making up

6 Tack a line 12 mm (½ in) on either side of the embroidery. This will be the finished width of the tieback. Add a 4 cm (1½ in) hem allowance outside the tacked lines and trim the fabric.

7 Turn under, press and tack a double 12 mm (½ in) hem along each edge. Draw out four threads beginning at the edge of the hem on both sides.

8 Work hemstitch from the right side along each hem edge, gathering the fabric threads into bundles of four. Check that you are catching the hem in on the reverse side as you stitch.

9 Work hemstitch along the inner edge of the drawn threads. Work the stitches exactly opposite so the fabric threads form bars.

10 Press the ends of the tiebacks into a point. Trim the fabric outside the crease line to 4 cm (1½ in). Turn under, press and tack a double 12 mm (½ in) hem along each edge. Slipstitch the hem in place.

11 Stitch a small curtain ring at each end of the tieback on the reverse side. For a professional finish, stitch the ring that will be the front of the tie back 12 mm (½ in) back from the point. Stitch the back ring jutting halfway out over the point.

12 To fit the tieback, hook the back ring on the hook and bring the tieback around the curtain. Hook the front of the tieback in place. To draw the curtains, you only need to lift the front ring off and let the tiebacks fall down behind the curtain.

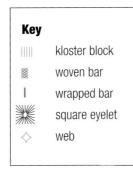

Key

‖‖‖	kloster block
▦	woven bar
ǀ	wrapped bar
✳	square eyelet
◇	web

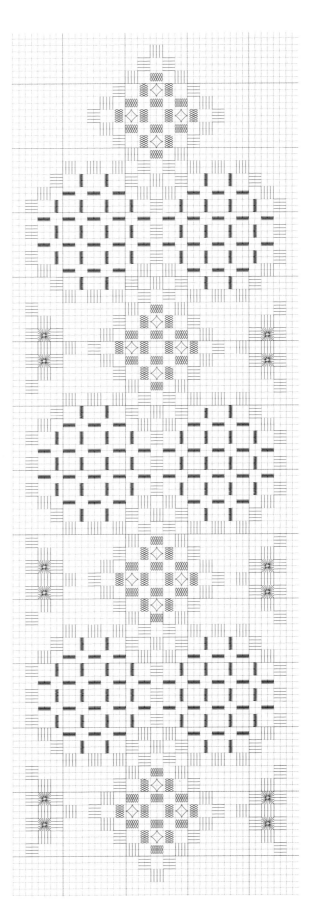

Window Blind

Blinds or flat curtains can be used to screen an unattractive view or to provide privacy at a window that looks out onto the street. The lace effect of Hardanger embroidery shows up well against the window, the light enhancing its detail, and the shaped buttonhole edging is much prettier than a straight edge.

This permanent flat blind hangs part way down the window. To find the finished width of the blind, measure inside the recess and take off 2 cm (¾ in) for ease of movement. For a blind that hangs outside the recess, allow an overlap of 5 cm (2 in) on each side. Work out how many repeats will fit across the bottom edge of the blind. For an uneven number of repeats, work the same part repeat on each side to fill the finished width.

Key

‖‖‖	kloster block
▓	picot bar
◲	buttonhole stitch
⌇	satin stitch

Working the Hardanger

1 Cut a piece of Davosa fabric 5 cm (2 in) longer and wider than required. Tack a line 20 cm (8 in) from the bottom of the evenweave fabric and mark the centre.

2 Using no. 3 perlé, work a heart-shaped satin stitch motif in the centre just below the line. Complete the zigzag satin stitch pattern. For an even number of repeats, the centre heart motif will be at the point of the zigzag; with an odd number of repeats the centre heart will be inbetween.

3 When the satin stitch is complete, work the kloster blocks in no. 3 perlé as shown in the chart. Cut the four threads at the end of each kloster block and pull the threads out. If you are at all unsure which threads to cut, refer back to the techniques section on page 16.

4 Using no. 5 perlé, work woven bars with picots on all thread bars.

5 Count the threads carefully to begin stitching the buttonhole border in no. 3 perlé. Once complete, cut the excess fabric along the bottom edge carefully. Use small pointed scissors.

Making up

6 Once the stitching is complete, trim the side seams 2 cm (¾ in) away from the stitching. Fold and press a 1 cm (⅜ in) double hem down both sides. Tack the hems and then machine-stitch.

7 Check the length of the blind against the window and trim it 2 cm (¾ in) longer than required. To finish the top edge, turn under the hem allowance and press. Pin a length of the loop side of the Velcro to the top edge of the blind, covering the raw edges, and machine-stitch in place.

8 Paint the wooden baton to match the window frame and attach it along the top of the window with screws. Attach the hook side of the Velcro to the front of the wooden baton. Carefully press the two pieces of Velcro together to stick the blind in place.

Fire Screen

A fire screen stands on the hearth in front of the fireplace, hiding the empty grate when the fire isn't in use. Choose the linen to match the room's décor and back in a contrast fabric to emphasize the cutwork.

Fire screens come in many shapes and sizes, so measure carefully to ensure that the stitching is the correct size and that it will be positioned correctly. You can choose a finer or coarser fabric to alter the size of the stitching if required. Allow plenty of fabric on either side of the stitching if the fire screen resembles a picture frame, as you will need to stretch the fabric around a piece of mount board. There are fire regulations to cover bought home furnishings and it is recommended that you spray the fabric with a fire retardant spray before use.

The making up instructions will help you to fit the Hardanger to any fire screen that has two dowels or rods between the uprights. For any other style, refer to the manufacturer's instructions. The fire screen is very easy to make using 2.5 cm (1 in) square lengths of wood, and any carpenter will be able to make a similar design if required. The wood is stained black and finished with a black patina wax.

Working the Hardanger

1 Cut the evenweave fabric at least 5 cm (2 in) larger than required and tack a line to mark the required finished size in the centre of the fabric. Tack a line vertically down the centre.

2 Measure the depth of the design on the evenweave fabric, allowing for a plain fabric border inside the tacked line. Begin in the centre and work the kloster blocks in no. 5 perlé. Work the zigzag line first, then count the threads very carefully to stitch the large diamond. Work the small diamonds.

3 Count the threads carefully and stitch the cable stitch zigzag lines with either nos. 5 or 8 perlé. The thicker thread produces a solid line similar to backstitch and the finer thread creates a pulled stitch with small holes visible between the stitches.

4 To remove the threads in the diamond motifs, cut four fabric threads across the end of each kloster block. On the crenellated-edge squares, cut four threads and then leave the next four. Cut the last four threads and repeat on each side. Pull the threads out very carefully.

5 Using no. 8 perlé, work double wrapped bars across the thread bars on all the cut motifs. Carefully following the chart on the right, stitch a single thread across the cut squares on the crenellated-edge motifs. Note that the direction of the single threads alternates on adjacent motifs.

Making up

6 Stitch the Hardanger on the evenweave fabric to the exact width required. Measure the length between the outside edges of the dowels and add 2 cm (¾ in) turning allowance. Trim the sides leaving a 1.5 cm (⅝ in) seam allowance.

7 Cut a piece of fabric exactly the same size and pin to the Hardanger with right sides together. Machine-stitch from the linen side, stitching along a thread of linen. Leave a gap along the bottom edge for turning.

8 Zigzag the seam allowance where the Hardanger border touches the side seam. Neatly trim close to the stitches. Trim across the corners and turn through.

9 Ease out the corners and press the seams. Slipstitch the gap. Stick the top and bottom edges to the dowel using double-sided tape. Secure in place on the fire screen with strong tape or fine staples.

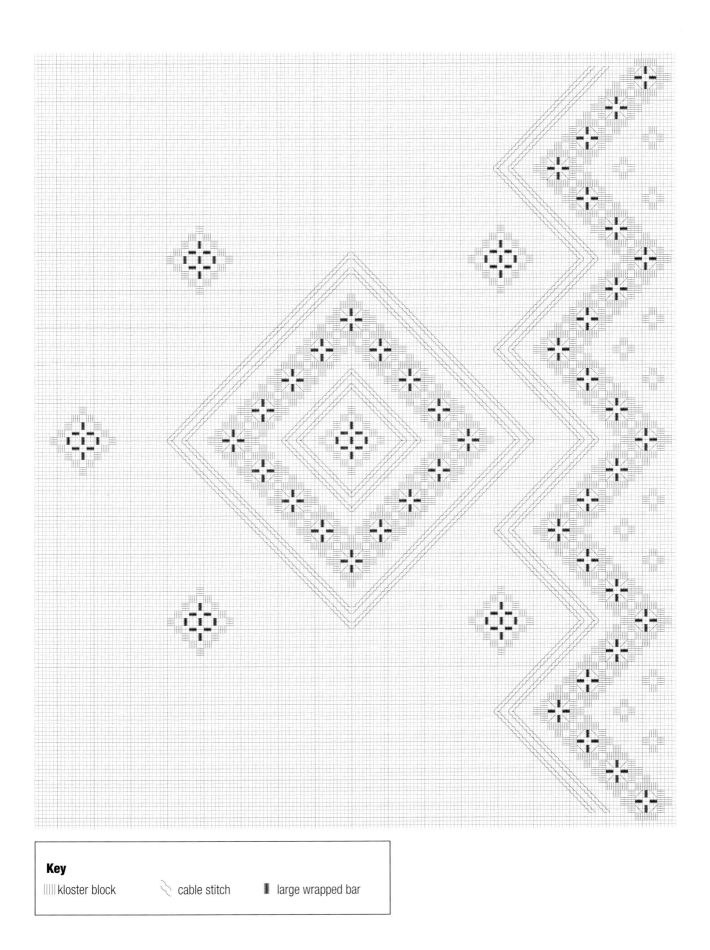

Key

||||| kloster block   ⌇ cable stitch   ▊ large wrapped bar

Window Hangings

The intricate cutwork in Hardanger shows up beautifully when held up against the light. These window hangings, made in contrasting shades of raw and bleached Dublin linen, are quite exquisite. Dublin linen is woven from tightly spun linen with a loose open weave that gives the fabric a translucent, delicate appearance. The woven bars and picots make a delightful but simple design inside the heart shape.

The fabric is stretched over a length of galvanized wire which has been bent into a heart shape and wrapped with tape. Round lampshade rings would also be suitable to make an alternative shape for the hangings.

You will need to stitch the Hardanger very carefully. Avoid carrying the thread across any areas of plain linen and keep the back of the work tidy by trimming the ends of threads neatly so that no stray threads will be visible when the stitching is held up to the light.

YOU WILL NEED:
Evenweave fabric: Dublin linen in
   white and natural
DMC perlé: white and soft brown
   642 nos. 5 and 8
Sewing kit
Galvanized wire
Fine silver wire
Wire cutters
Narrow white cotton tape
Fine ribbon or cord for hanging

Finished size of stitching:
Depth: 10 cm (4 in)
Width: 12 cm (4¾ in)

Finished size of hanging:
16 x 16 cm (6¼ x 6¼ in)

Working the Hardanger

1 Cut a piece of linen 20 cm
(8 in) square and tack lines
across the centre of the linen
horizontally and vertically. Insert
pins to mark the finished size of
the stitching and tack.

2 Begin in the centre at the
bottom point of the heart and
work the kloster blocks in no. 5
perlé. If you do not meet the
point again exactly on the other
side, you have made a mistake
stitching and counting the
threads. Check each block
carefully and unpick up to the
mistake. Re-stitch to make a
perfect heart. Work square eyelets
around the edge as shown.

3 Cut the threads at the end of
the remaining kloster blocks. If
you are unsure which threads to
cut, refer to the techniques section
on page 16. Pull the cut threads
out carefully.

4 Using no. 8 perlé, work woven
bars with picots along all the
thread bars.

Making up

5 Cut a 75 cm (30 in) length of
galvanized wire, and bend in half.
Curve the sides into a heart shape
16 cm (6¼ in) in depth. Adjust
the curves to echo the shape of
the stitched heart, leaving a 2 cm
(¾ in) border around the
Hardanger stitching.

6 Cut the ends of the galvanized
wire and wrap with the silver wire
to secure. Wrap the wire heart
with the narrow tape, wrapping at
an angle and overlapping half the
tape each time. Stitch the end of
the tape neatly.

7 Lay the wrapped heart shape
over the Hardanger stitching on
the reverse side and draw a line
6 mm (¼ in) away. Zigzag around
the outside of the marked line.
Trim the fabric close to the
stitching.

8 Replace the heart on the
reverse side of the linen and pin
the fabric over the wire. Working
from the right side, oversew with
alternate straight and diagonal
stitches using a no. 8 perlé. Attach
a length of no. 5 perlé or ribbon
to the top of the heart for
hanging.

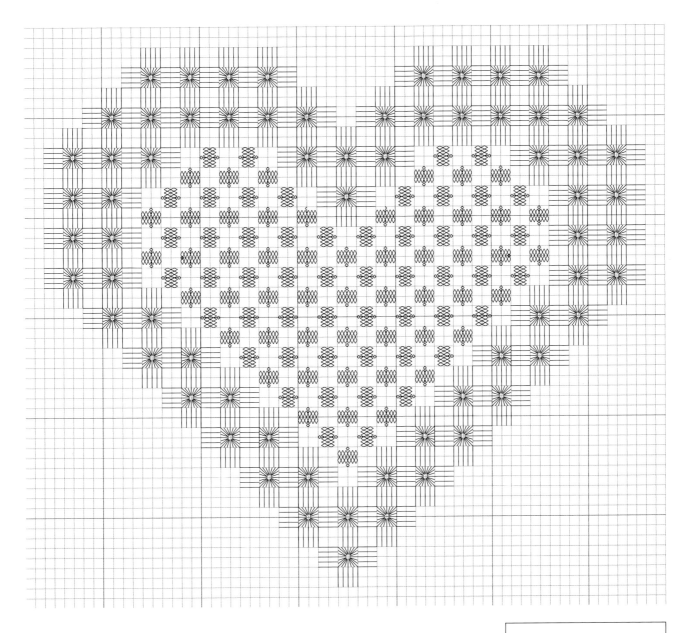

Key
| | | | | kloster block

picot bars

square eyelet

The dining room offers many opportunities for Hardanger embroidery. Lay tablecloths, mats and table centres directly on a dark wood table or place a contrasting table cover underneath to enhance the beauty of the embroidered cutwork. Stitch these designs in traditional white and cream or choose one of the brightly coloured linens available today, such as the red fabric used here for table napkins.

in the DINING ROOM

Table Runner

A pure white linen table runner is one of the most elegant table coverings and looks stunning set down the centre of a plain wooden table. A table runner can be used as a means of decorating a table when not in use, or makes a useful continuous tablemat for dinner parties. It can be made to fit the length of the table or be long enough to hang down at each end.

I have used a cotton/viscose mix fabric called Lugana here as it launders well and is easier to press than pure linen. The viscose content adds a slight sheen and has better draping qualities than pure cotton. Spray the 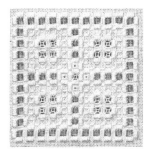 runner with starch before pressing for a really crisp finish.

You could also stitch the small squares from the centre motif in the corner of 40 cm (16 in) squares of Lugana to make a set of matching napkins, or stitch the large square in the middle of 30 × 40 cm (12 × 16 in) pieces of linen for tablemats. The white on white design is classic, but it could be stitched on any colour of fabric.

YOU WILL NEED:
Evenweave fabric: Lugana in
   white
DMC perlé: white nos. 5 and 8
Sewing kit

Finished size of stitching:
Depth of border: 9 cm (3½ in)
Width of one repeat: 30 cm
   (12 in)

Finished size of table runner:
Finished width: 40 cm (16 in). Add
   8 cm (3 in) for side hems and
   20 cm (8 in) for the end hems

Working the Hardanger

1 Cut the linen fabric 5 cm (2 in) larger than required. Tack a line 30 cm (12 in) from each end and mark the centre of the fabric. Count the fabric threads carefully and stitch the kloster blocks for the centre motif above the line at each end. Work the square kloster blocks for the large square on either side. using no. 5 perlé.

2 Using no. 8 perlé, stitch the marked backstitch lines between the kloster blocks as shown on the chart on the right. Holbein stitch looks similar to backstitch but has a better finish for this design.

3 Cut the threads at the end of each kloster block on the centre motif and carefully pull out the threads. If you are unsure where to cut the threads, refer to the techniques section on page 16. Cut into the threads at the end of each border on the large squares and carefully pull the threads out. Cut the threads at the end of each kloster block all the way round the border to create small cut squares.

4 Work woven bars across all the thread bars, using no. 8 perlé. Complete the Hardanger design with lace stitch (square web) worked as indicated on the chart.

Making up

5 Mark the finished size of the runner on the stitched evenweave fabric. Carefully measure the hem allowances on each edge and cut the fabric to size. Turn under, press and tack a double 2 cm (¾ in) hem down each side. Turn up, press and tack a double 5 cm (2 in) hem at each end, taking great care to fold the hem exactly along a thread of the fabric.

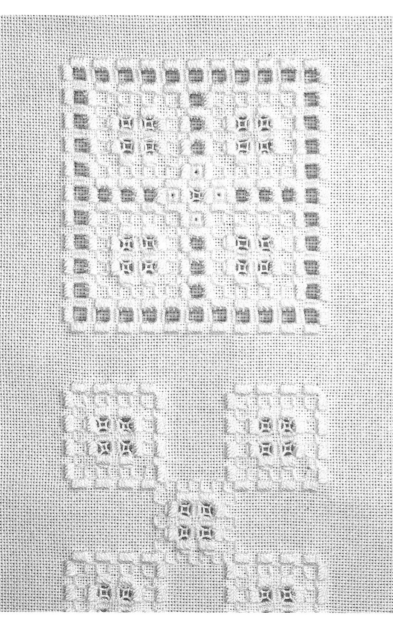

6 Cut and draw two threads on the main fabric level with the top of the hem. Only draw the threads out as far as the side hems. Draw out two threads down each side seam in the same way.

7 Trim the drawn threads back to 1 cm (½ in) and tuck them inside the hem. Work hemstitch from the reverse side, catching in the hem as you go.

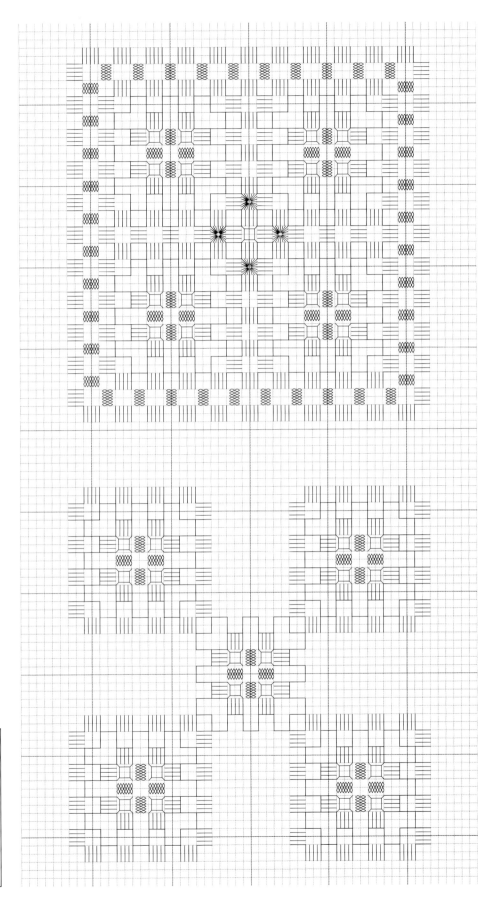

Key

‖‖‖	kloster block
▨	woven bar
✴	square eyelet
⌐	backstitch
⊓	square web

Tablemat and Coaster

This set of tablemat and matching coaster is decorated with leaf shapes which are common in traditional Hardanger but not often seen elsewhere. Use a contrast thread for the leaf shapes so they stand out from the background.

As table linen is frequently laundered, use a firmly woven fabric such as Hardanger which is unlikely to fray in the wash. Unlike other evenweave fabrics, the satin stitches are worked between the pairs of threads and over four pairs rather than over four threads only. As a result, it is a quick fabric to stitch on. Similar count fabrics, such as Bellana, have too loose a weave for these large cut squares. The finest fabric I would recommend for this design is Lugana.

Working the Hardanger

1 For the tablemat, cut a piece of Hardanger fabric 30 × 43 cm (12 × 17 in). Tack the finished size of the tablemat in the centre of the fabric. Mark the position of the border with pins and tack just outside the line.

2 Work the grid of kloster blocks inside the marked rectangle using ecru no. 5 perlé. The squares and rectangles are created from groups of nine satin stitches with four fabric threads in between.

3 Beginning at the corner, cut eight threads, leave four and cut the remaining eight to complete the side. Cut the threads in the same way on each side and pull the threads out very carefully. On the rectangles, cut across the eight threads at the end of the kloster blocks and carefully pull out the threads to leave a bar down the centre.

4 Weave all the thread bars using ecru no. 8 perlé.

5 Follow the diagram in the technique section to help you work the leaf. Using white no. 8 perlé, stitch two threads across the first cut square. Stitch a further two threads, slightly loose, one on each side of the centre stitches. Support the threads with your finger from the underside and begin to weave across the threads. As you continue to weave, keep the stitches quite loose so that the woven bar widens gradually. As you pass the centre point make each stitch slightly smaller to create the leaf shape. Work a leaf shape in each of the cut squares.

6 The loops either side of the thread bar in the rectangle are worked in Shuttle stitch, using ecru no. 8 perlé. This is similar to buttonhole stitch but the stitches are worked in pairs so that the thread bar doesn't twist. Use the

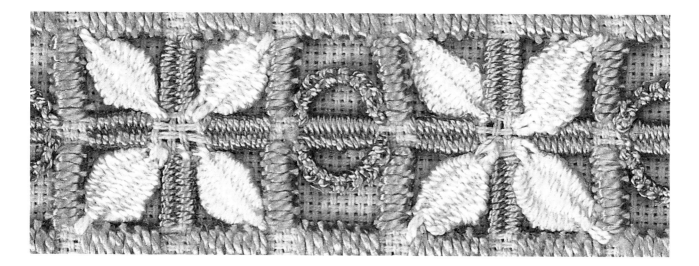

diagrams in the techniques section on page 21 to help you work the stitch. Using no. 8 perlé, make two loose loops either side of the bar. Work a buttonhole stitch in the normal way and then take the needle under the thread bars and back under the working thread to form the Shuttle stitch. Fill both bars with stitches to create two semi-circles.

Making up

7 Trim the fabric along a thread, 2 cm (¾ in) out from the finished size tacked line. Turn under and press a double 1 cm (⅜ in) hem. Mitre the corners.

8 Tack the hem in position. Snip and draw out two threads around the edge of the hem. Neatly trim the thread ends and tuck inside the hem. Work hemstitch from the reverse side using a matching sewing cotton.

Key

|||||	kloster block
▨	woven bar
⟨	shuttle stitch
⬭	leaf shape

Tablecloth

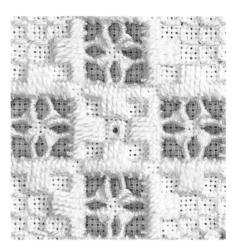

Table settings for special occasions require that little bit of extra effort and a beautiful tablecloth is one of the easiest ways to begin. Table linen is traditionally made from pure linen and there is a huge range of evenweave linen fabrics such as Belfast, Cork and Dublin linen available in a wide range of colours which look stunning when starched and pressed.

If you are looking for a fabric that is easier to launder and press, try one of the mixed fibre evenweaves such as Quaker, which is a mix of cotton and linen. The fabric I have used here, Lugana, is a cotton/viscose mix. It is one of the most popular choices for Hardanger because it is easy to stitch on but also looks quite fine.

The design for this tablecloth can be adapted to suit any shape or size of table. There is a central motif and a different corner motif. The corner motifs can be placed at regular intervals along the edge of the table if it is rectangular rather than square. For a larger table, lines of drawn thread work can be worked across the cloth midway between the motifs. Finish the edge of the cloth with a narrow machine-stitched hem or a deeper drawn thread hem.

YOU WILL NEED:
Evenweave fabric: Lugana in
    white
DMC perlé: white nos. 5 and 8
Sewing kit

Finished size of stitching:
Corner squares: 13 cm (5 in)
Centre motif: 19 cm (7½ in)

Finished size of tablecloth:
135 x 135 cm (53 x 53 in)

Working the Hardanger

1 To work out the finished size
of the tablecloth to suit your
table, measure across the table to
find the width and length and
add the required drop and hem
allowance to each edge. Unless
you want the tablecloth to reach
right down to the floor, the drop
is the distance between the
tabletop and your knees as you
sit at the table. Add 12 mm
(½ in) to each edge for a narrow
machine hem or add twice the
hem width for a deep mitred
hem (see page 25). Cut the fabric
slightly larger and zigzag the

edges on the sewing machine to
prevent them fraying.

2 Lay the fabric over the table
and line the straight grain of the
fabric with the edge of the table.
Measure to find the centre of the
table and insert pins to mark its
position on the tablecloth. Mark
the corners of the table on the
tablecloth.

3 Tack a 13 cm (5 in) square at
each corner and a 19 cm (7½ in)
square in the centre. Using no. 5
perlé, work the kloster block
border and crenellated edge
motifs inside the tacked lines,
following the chart on the left for
the corners and on the right for
the central design.

4 Using no. 8 perlé, fill the
background area around the satin
stitches with backstitch and work
the eyelets as indicated on the
chart on the right.

5 Cut the first four threads, leave
four and cut the last four threads
on each side of the crenellated
edge motifs. Pull out the threads
very carefully. Using no. 8 perlé,
work adjoining wrap in each of
the cut squares, following the
diagram in the techniques section
on page 20. Cut the threads
inside each group of kloster blocks
around the border to form a series
of square holes.

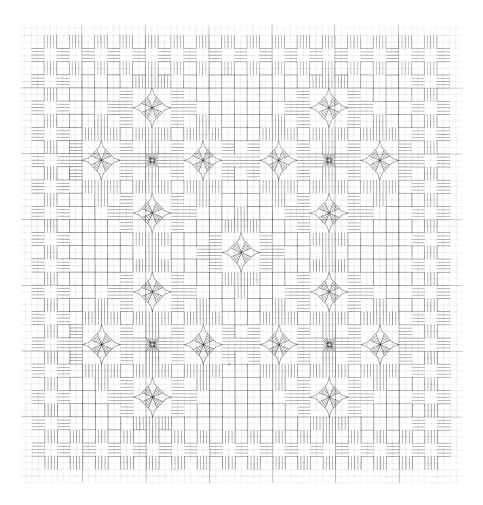

Making up

6 Trim the edge of the tablecloth along a thread to get it exactly straight. To make the hem, turn under 6 mm (¼ in) along each side and press. Trim a small square from each corner along the crease lines to reduce bulk. Fold the hem

over a further 6 mm (¼ in) down two sides and machine-stitch close to the inside fold.

7 Turn under the top and bottom edges and machine-stitch in the same way. See the techniques section on page 25 if you prefer to work a deeper hem.

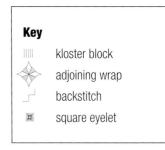

Key

‖‖	kloster block
◇	adjoining wrap
⌐	backstitch
▦	square eyelet

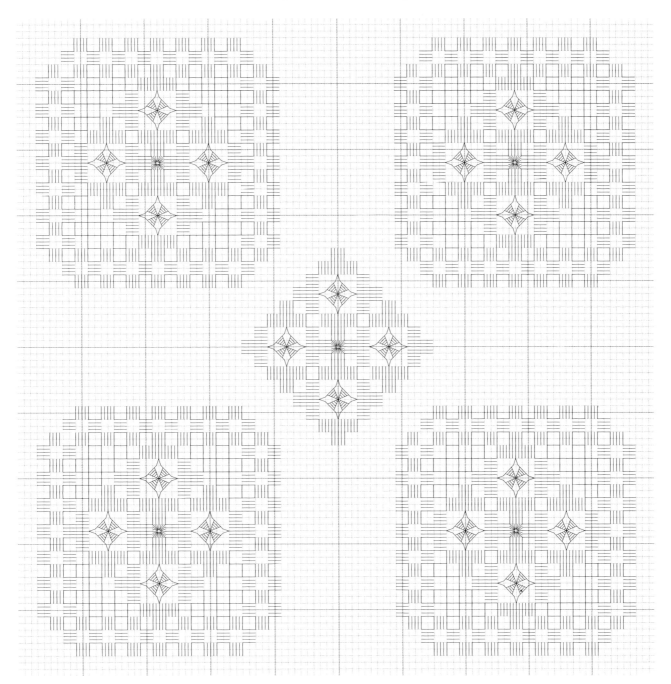

Linen Napkins

Linen napkins are practical as well as beautiful, and should not necessarily be kept for special occasions only. It is a good idea to give everyone his or her own napkin for everyday use which can then be rolled up and stored in a drawer between meals. You could give each person a different napkin ring to identify their own napkin.

These bright napkins will cheer up any table and shouldn't need to be washed every day. At 32 count, Belfast linen is the finest linen that you can comfortably stitch without a magnifying lamp. It is available in a wide range of colours as well as white and cream. If you decide to stitch on coarser linen or an easy-care fabric such as Lugana, the motif will probably be too big for a napkin. Either stitch the cutwork or just one of the satin stitch stars instead.

You can use the design to create matching table linen, stitching four stars around the diamond motif for a table centre or tablemat or a row of stars to make a napkin ring. I used a subtly variegated thread to stitch the Hardanger embroidery, separating the thread into lengths of light and dark shades. The Kloster blocks are worked in the darker threads, the stars in the lighter shade.

Working the Hardanger

1 Cut a 50 cm (20 in) square of linen for each napkin and zigzag the edge on the sewing machine to prevent fraying. Tack a line 4 cm (1½ in) in along each edge to mark the finished size.

2 Tack a 12 cm (4¾ in) square, 5 cm (2 in) in from the tacked line on one corner to show where to work the Hardanger design.

3 To divide the no. 8 variegated perlé thread into lengths of light and dark threads, reel off the thread and form it into a circle. You will find that the colour shades from light to dark in a uniform manner and you can lay the threads down so that the light shades all lie together. Cut the circle in half so the light shades appear on one side and the dark on the other.

4 Use the lighter threads to work the satin stitch, beginning with a star in the corner of the tacked square. Count the threads carefully and then stitch the kloster blocks on the diamond motif using the darker lengths of thread.

5 Using the no. 12 pink perlé, work the eyelets as indicated on the chart shown on the right. Work the cable stitch diamond using no. 8 variegated perlé.

6 Cut out the centres of the kloster blocks and work dove's eye filling (web) in each cut square using the no. 12 pink perlé.

Making up

7 Trim the napkin to 45 cm (18 in) and complete a narrow machine-stitched hem around the edge.

8 To make the hem, turn under 6 mm (¼ in) along each side and press. Trim a small square from each corner along the crease lines to reduce bulk. Fold the hem over a further 6 mm (¼ in) down two sides and machine-stitch close to the inside fold. Turn under the top and bottom edges and machine-stitch in the same way.

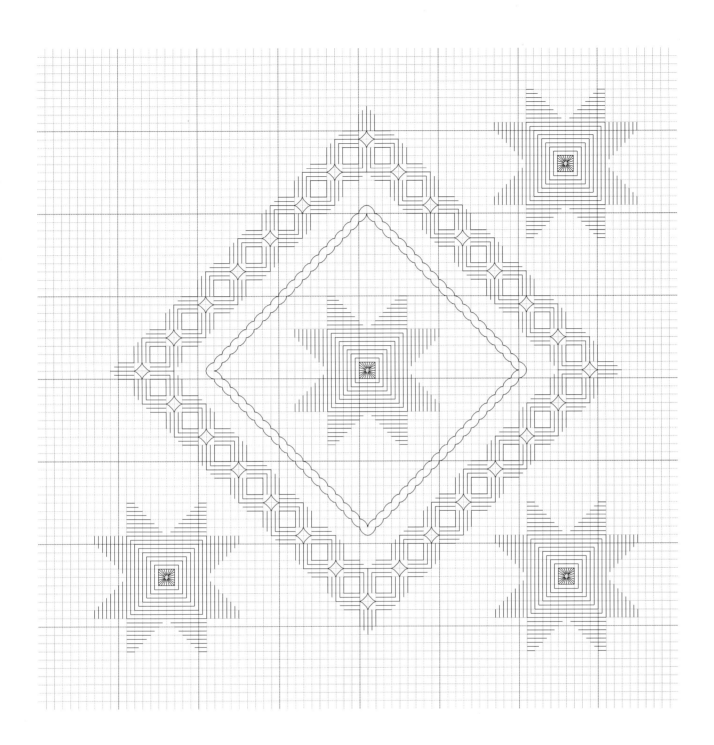

Key

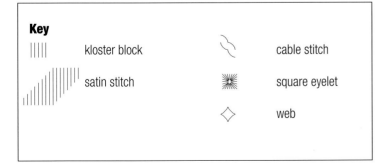

‖‖‖	kloster block	
(satin pattern)	satin stitch	
∿	cable stitch	
✳	square eyelet	
◇	web	

Table Centre

The beauty of a table centre is that it will fit any size or shape of table and is ideal to give as a gift. It can be placed directly onto a wooden table or over a coloured tablecloth for contrast. This particular design is 51 cm (20 in) in

diameter and would look stunning as a tablemat over a floor-length cover on a circular side table. The design can also be stitched in the centre of a full-sized cloth.

I chose to stitch the table centre on Damask Hardanger because it is such a beautiful fabric with a wonderful sheen. The weave of the fabric is not distinct and I found that it is much easier to work if you have a magnifying lamp. Because there is no centre motif and the design is circular, you do need to count the threads between the motifs very carefully otherwise the design will not match at the other side. If you are a beginner, use a fabric that is much easier to count, such as regular Hardanger or Bellana. Stitch the small diamond motif in the corner of napkins to make a matching set of table linen.

Working the Hardanger

1 Cut a piece of Damask Hardanger, at least 61 cm (24 in) square. Fold it in four to find the centre and mark with a pin. Tack lines across the centre, horizontally and vertically, using small stitches.

2 Measure 9 cm (3½ in) from the centre point along one of the tacked lines. This is the corner of one of the square motifs. Using a no. 5 perlé, stitch the outside row of kloster blocks only. Count the threads very carefully to stitch the outside row of kloster blocks on the adjacent motif. Continue around the design, only stitching the outside row of the pattern at this stage. This is a precautionary measure – there will be less to unpick if you miscount!

3 Once the circle of kloster block borders are complete and you are satisfied that the spacing is exact, work the kloster blocks in the centre of each square.

4 Using no. 5 perlé, stitch the backstitch lines between the kloster blocks. Use Holbein stitch, rather than backstitch, to achieve a more even result. Stitch the backstitch lines around the outer edge in the same way.

5 Cut the threads at the end of the kloster blocks in the centre of the square motifs. If you are unsure where to cut, refer to the techniques section. Pull the threads out carefully.

6 Using a no. 8 perlé, weave the thread bars. Work four webs in the centre of each motif as indicated on the chart to complete the design.

Making up

7 To finish the hem of the table centre, work buttonhole stitch in no. 5 perlé around the outside edge as indicated on the chart. Begin at one of the tacked lines and count very carefully as you go. Check at each tacked line that you have not miscounted.

8 Cut the excess fabric outside the buttonhole stitch to finish.

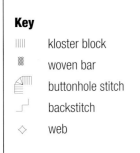

Key

|||||	kloster block
▨	woven bar
◁⊓⊓	buttonhole stitch
⌐	backstitch
◇	web

The bedroom is the ideal place to create a romantic mood, and using Hardanger embroidery is the perfect way to achieve this. Use pure white linen to stitch an exquisite pillowcase or lavender sachet, or choose a pretty coloured fabric to make a dressing table mat or shelf border. Alternatively, make the bed the focal point of the room by adding a stunning Hardanger border to a plain duvet cover.

in the
BEDROOM

Linen Pillowcase

Pure linen is the ultimate luxury fabric for bedlinen and is ideal for an Oxford-style pillowcase because the fabric can be starched to hold the shape of the flange around the edge. This pillowcase is unashamedly decorative and is designed to sit on top of the bedcovers during the day and to be lifted to one side at night. If you want to stitch a pillowcase for sleeping on, keep the Hardanger embroidery to the outside edge so that your face will not be lying against the stitching – larger square pillows have plenty of room for the design around the edge.

Oxford-style pillowcases are quick and easy to make, even with the most basic sewing machine, as you only need straight stitch. It is easier to make up the pillowcases after stitching the Hardanger so the embroidery can be worked on the flat fabric. It is essential to shrink the linen before you begin: hand-wash it in warm water with some fabric softener; roll in a towel to remove excess moisture and then press until the fabric is dry.

Working the Hardanger

1 Assuming the pillow is 48×68 cm (19×27 in), cut a piece of linen 66×110 cm (26×43 in) for the front and flap of the pillowcase and zigzag around the edge to prevent fraying. Beginning in a corner, 2.5 cm (1 in) from each edge, tack an outline 61×81 cm (24×32 in) to indicate the finished size of the pillow on the fabric. Tack a second line 5 cm (2 in) further in for the flange. There will be at least 23 cm (9 in) spare fabric for the flap at the other end.

2 Mark the centre of the pillowcase and tack lines out in both directions along a thread. Stitch the centre square first. The large squares have 85 satin stitches on each side. Double-check there are the correct number of stitches on each side otherwise the design will not fit inside.

3 Measure 7.5 cm (3 in) to either side, then work the satin stitch edge in no. 5 perlé for the other large squares. Stitch a small square in the centre, 5 cm (2 in) above and below the large squares. There are 37 satin stitches on each side of the small squares.

4 For the large squares, cut four threads and leave twelve. Continue along each side, finishing with four cut threads in each corner. Pull the threads out carefully. Cut the four threads next to the corners on each of the small squares, leave threads on either side and cut the centre four.

5 Using no. 8 perlé, work three woven bars over the twelve threads on each side of the squares. Follow the chart carefully – there are regular woven bars in the centre of each small square and a woven bar with a picot on the outside edge only.

Making up

6 Assuming the pillow is 48×68 cm (19×27 in), cut a piece of linen 61×81 cm (24×32 in) for the back. Fold and

stitch a 1.5 cm (⅝ in) double hem along one short side of the back.

7 On the pillowcase front, trim the seam allowance outside the tacked line to 1.5 cm (⅝ in) down the side. Trim the seam allowance on the two long sides to the same size, continuing along the sides of the flap. Trim the zigzag edge of the flap. Turn under a 1.5 cm (⅝ in) double hem along the edge of the flap.

8 With wrong sides together, fold the flap along the tacked line and pin along the side seams. Position the back panel 5 cm (2 in) from the folded edge and pin. Machine-stitch and trim the seam allowances to 6 mm (¼ in). Turn the pillowcase through and roll the edge between your fingers. Ease out the corners and press.

9 On the sewing machine, measure 5 cm (2 in) from the needle and stick a piece of masking tape onto the needle plate to mark the width of the flange. Using the tape as a guide, topstitch the border to complete the pillowcase.

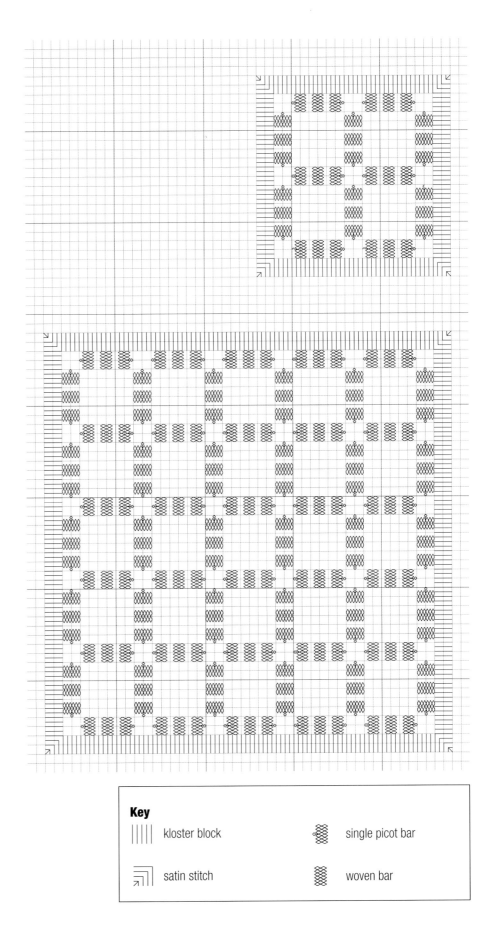

Key

‖‖‖	kloster block	✕	single picot bar
satin stitch		✕	woven bar

Lavender Sachet

This exquisite lavender sachet is ideal to make for a gift or for your own underwear drawer. It can be filled with a small muslin bag filled with lavender or pot pourri. The lavender sachet is simply a strip of fabric, with the Hardanger stitched at one end. The fabric is folded up and stitched down the side seams to make a little pouch. To make it even prettier, find a beautiful shell button to stitch beneath the flap.

Belfast linen is about the finest linen that can be used for Hardanger because of the difficulty of counting and cutting the threads. It is much easier to stitch and cut threads on Belfast linen using a magnifying lamp. If coarser linen is chosen, the design can be used to make a larger bag for holding handkerchiefs or jewellery. For example, the bag would be 18 cm (7 in) square if stitched on Dublin linen and almost twice the size at 24 cm (9½ in) if the design were stitched on Davosa instead. If you decide to use a different fabric remember to use thicker thread: Dublin is stitched with nos. 5 and 8 coton perlé and Davosa with nos. 3 and 5.

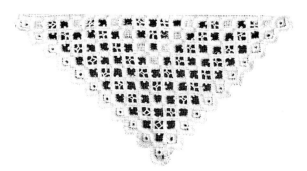

YOU WILL NEED:
Evenweave fabric: Belfast linen
  in white
DMC perlé: white nos. 8 and 12
Sewing kit

Finished size of stitching:
13.5 x 7 cm (5½ x 2¾ in)

Finished size of sachet:
13.5 x 13 cm (5½ x 5 in)

Working the Hardanger

1 Cut an 18 × 40 cm (6 × 16 in) piece of linen. Tack a line 10 cm (4 in) from one end of the fabric. Using no. 8 perlé, stitch the top row of kloster blocks just inside the line. Continue stitching the remaining kloster blocks over the rest of the design.

2 Using no. 8 perlé, work the buttonhole stitch border around the bottom edge of the design. Work an eyelet in each fabric square along the buttonhole edge using no. 12 perlé.

3 Cut the threads at the end of the satin stitches referring to the chart to see where to cut. If you are unsure which threads to cut, refer to the technique section at the beginning of the book. Pull the threads out carefully.

4 Using no. 12 perlé, weave the thread bars using the woven bars with a single picot on one side. The chart shows which side to stitch the picot.

5 Using the chart as a guide, work Dove's eye filling (web) using no. 12 perlé.

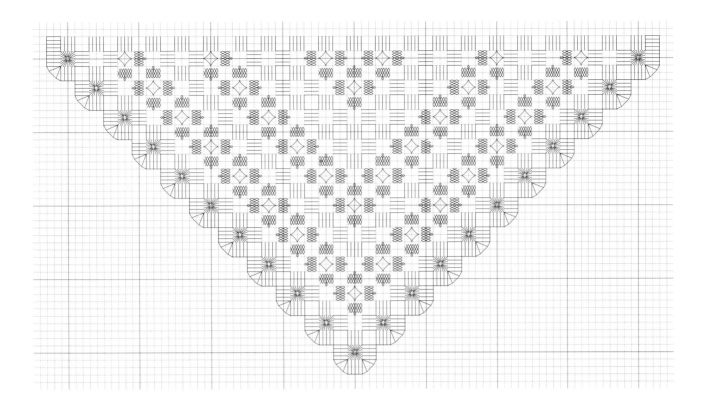

Making up

6 Trim the excess fabric from around the buttonhole edge only. Fold the fabric in three to make a 12 cm (4¾ in) deep sachet shape. Fold the hem of the inside flap level with the top of the Hardanger. Trim to 12 mm (½ in). Press 6 mm (¼ in) along the edge and fold over again to the reverse side to make a double hem. Machine-stitch.

7 Fold the sachet up with the right sides together. Machine-stitch the side seams. Zigzag the seams close to the previous stitching and trim neatly.

8 Turn the sachet through and ease out the corners. Sew a small buttonhole loop at the point of the flap large enough to just fit around the button. Stitch the button in position on the front of the sachet.

Key	
‖‖‖	kloster block
▓	single picot bar
◲	buttonhole stitch
✳	square eyelet
◇	web

Dressing Table Set

T his pretty set would look delightful on any dressing table. Satin stitch is a feature of Hardanger embroidery and the traditional tulip motif is one of the most popular designs.

Finish the mat with a simple narrow machine hem or make a wider hem with mitred corners. The wider hem can be machine-stitched or, for a more decorative finish, hand-stitched using drawn thread work. This is another counted thread technique that is often used to create the hems on Hardanger embroidery. Threads are cut and pulled out along the inside edge of the hem and then the remaining threads are stitched into groups of three or four to create a delicate edge.

Working the Hardanger

1 Cut a piece of linen approximately 45 × 56 cm (18 × 22 in). Zigzag the edges to prevent fraying. Tack the finished size of the mat so that there is an equal border on all sides.

2 Tack lines across the centre in both directions. Begin by working the cable stitch lines so that you can position the other motifs accurately. Measure 5 cm (2 in) along the tacked line from the centre and begin to stitch the cable stitch line using no. 5 perlé. Work all the cable stitch lines that criss-cross the mat.

3 Using no. 5 perlé, stitch the satin stitch tulips at the end of each line.

4 Count the threads and stitch the diamond shaped edging for the motifs with no. 5 perlé. Work the cable stitch as before around the individual motifs.

5 Cut six threads in each corner of the diamond motifs, leaving the centre four threads. Using no. 8 perlé, work woven bars with picots on each of the thread bars.

6 To complete the design, stitch a single thread across each of the cut squares using no. 5 perlé.

Making up

7 Measure 6 cm (2½ in) out from the tacked line and cut along a thread. Fold a double 3 cm (1¼ in) hem and press. Mitre the corners and tack the hem in position.

8 Cut across two threads on each side next to the hem and draw out as far as the inside corner. Trim the ends and tuck inside the hem.

9 Work hemstitch from the inside along each edge of the hem gathering threads into bundles of four. Slipstitch the mitred corners.

10 Follow the manufacturer's instructions to insert the small design into the trinket pot lid.

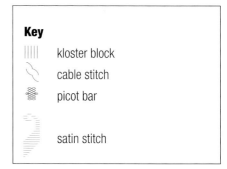

Key

||||| kloster block

〰   cable stitch

▩   picot bar

   satin stitch

Duvet Cover

The bed is usually the largest item of furniture in the majority of bedrooms and fills much of the floor area. As a result, it is important to make the bedcover as attractive as possible. Plain duvet covers can be rather boring as there is such a large expanse of fabric so attach a deep decorative border across the duvet to break up the area.

Hardanger is an attractive technique to use for a border on a duvet cover as the cutwork allows the colour of the duvet to show through. This makes the border appear part of the cover rather than an addition. It is advisable to try out a small sample of the design on a piece of linen to check that it is suitable for the colour of the duvet cover as cream and ivory colours can be quite difficult to match. Stitch the zigzag pattern and attach along the edge of matching pillowcases to complete the set.

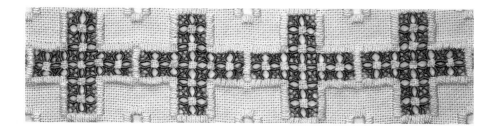

Working the Hardanger

1 Measure the width of the
duvet cover and work out the
number of repeats required to fit
across the width. Plan the repeats
so that if there will be only part of
the repeat, it will be the same size
at each side.

2 Cut a piece of fabric at least
5 cm (2 in) larger all round than
required. Fold the fabric into four
quarters to find the centre and
mark with a pin. If there is an odd
number of repeats, begin with a
cross motif in the centre, but with
an even number of repeats
position a cross either side of the
centre line. Using no. 5 ecru perlé,
work the satin stitches to create

the cross motifs. There are 13
stitches on each side of the motif.

3 Count the threads carefully
and work the zigzag line of kloster
blocks on either side of the centre
border, using ecru no. 5 perlé.
Complete the outside edge with
the buttonhole border.

4 Using soft brown no. 8 perlé,
work an eyelet in each of the
fabric squares along the
buttonhole border.

5 Cut the threads at the end of
the kloster blocks as indicated on
the chart. If you are unsure where
to cut the threads, refer to the
techniques section. Pull the
threads out carefully.

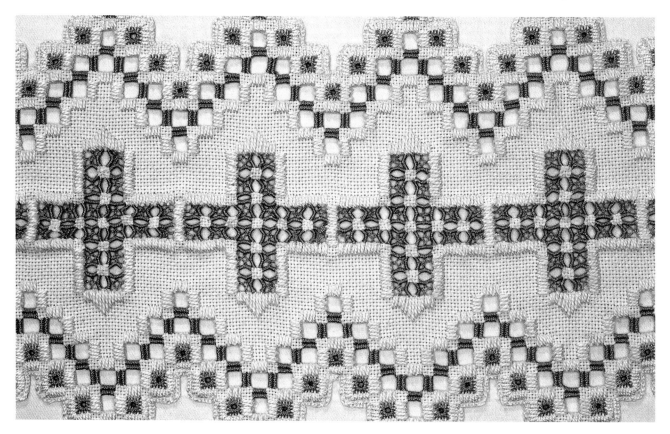

6 Wrap the thread bars along the border into groups of two. In the cross motifs wrap the thread bars, adding Dove's eye filling (web) in the chart as you go, using soft brown no. 8 perlé. Pull the Dove's eye filling stitches slightly tight to bend the wrapped bars in.

Making up

7 Cut the excess fabric along the edge of the buttonhole stitch, and leave a 1.5 cm (⅝ in) seam allowance at each end.

8 Unpick just enough of the side seams of the duvet cover to allow the Hardanger band to slot into place. Pin the embroidered fabric in position and tack carefully. Tuck the excess fabric into the side seams and re-sew.

9 Carefully stitch the Hardanger embroidery onto the duvet cover. Stitch by hand using backstitch or sew on the machine. Stitch around the edge of the buttonholing, keeping the stitches tucked in behind the bars on the outside edge.

Key	
‖‖‖	kloster block
▩	woven bar
◇	web
▨	square eyelet
◿▥	buttonhole stitch
∣	wrapped bar

Shelf Border

Shelf borders are a pretty way to finish the edges of wooden shelves, creating an instant country look. The border can be attached along an open shelf or on the inside of cupboards with glass doors. The depth of the border will depend on the space between the shelves, as a deep border could make access to the items on the shelf difficult.

You can simply attach the shelf border to the top of the shelf with a staple gun but it is much better to fix it to the front edge of the shelf with Velcro. Use a strip of non-adhesive soft loop Velcro to stitch to the top of the border and stick adhesive hook Velcro to the front of the shelf. This allows the border to be removed and laundered. If several shelves across the front of a window are fitted with deep shelf borders, they form a subtle window treatment, hiding an unattractive view yet still letting the light in.

YOU WILL NEED:
Evenweave fabric: Bellana in
    lavender 441
DMC perlé: white nos. 5 and 8
Sewing kit
Velcro

Finished size of stitching:
Depth of border: 11 cm (4¼ in)
Width of one repeat: 11.5 cm
    (4½ in)

**Finished depth of shelf
border:**
12 cm (4¾ in)

Working the Hardanger

1 Decide on the depth of the shelf border. The stitch area is 11 cm (4¼ in). Add an extra 5 cm (2 in) to the required depth for turnings and the excess below the stitching.

2 Measure the shelf and work out the number of repeats that will be required. If the design repeat is incomplete, try to make each end the same. Cut a strip of fabric 5 cm (2 in) longer than required and fold in half crossways. Tack a line to mark the centre.

3 If there is an odd number of repeats, begin with one of the large points on the centre line. With an even number of repeats, begin at one of the shorter points. Using no. 5 perlé, work the buttonhole border 2.5 cm (1 in) above the bottom raw edge, then stitch the kloster blocks to complete the design.

4 Using no. 8 perlé, stitch a large eyelet in the centre of the diamonds as indicated on the chart on the right.

5 Carefully cut the threads at the end of the kloster blocks. If

you are unsure which threads to cut, refer to page 16. Cut the centre from the small kloster block squares along the buttonhole border.

6 Using no. 8 perlé, wrap the thread bars in groups of two, working Dove's eye filling (web) as you go where it is indicated on the chart. Pull the Dove's eye filling stitch fairly tight to bend the wrapped bars slightly.

Making up

7 Cut the excess fabric below the buttonhole stitching and trim the ends of the shelf border to 1 cm (½ in). Make a 6 mm (¼ in) double hem and slipstitch.

8 Fold the top edge down to the reverse side and press. Pin a length of loop Velcro along the fold and machine-stitch.

9 Attach a self-adhesive hook Velcro strip to the front of the shelf. Stick the shelf border neatly in place.

Key	
‖‖‖	kloster block
‖	wrapped bars
◇	web
⌐	backstitch
✳	large eyelet
◿	buttonhole stitch

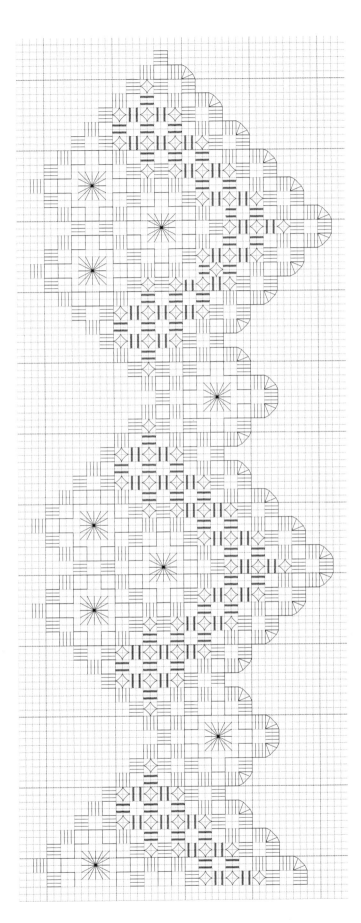

DMC Pearl Cotton

Key to colour numbers: shade number on left, column number on right.

ecru	17	317	18	519	7	730	11	831	11	955	9	3362	11	3809	7
blanc	17	318	18	520	10	731	11	832	11	956	2	3363	11	3810	7
b5200	17	319	9	522	10	732	11	833	11	957	2	3364	11	3811	7
48	19	320	9	523	10	733	11	834	11	958	7	3371	16	3812	7
51	20	321	1	524	10	734	11	838	16	959	7	3607	4	3813	8
52	19	322	6	535	17	738	16	839	16	961	2	3608	4	3814	8
53	20	326	2	543	16	739	16	840	16	962	2	3609	4	3815	8
57	19	327	4	550	4	740	13	841	16	963	2	3685	3	3816	8
61	20	333	5	552	4	741	13	842	16	964	7	3687	3	3817	8
62	19	334	6	553	4	742	13	844	17	966	9	3688	3	3818	9
67	19	335	2	554	4	743	13	869	12	970	13	3689	3	3819	11
69	20	336	6	561	8	744	13	890	9	971	13	3705	1	3820	12
75	19	340	5	562	8	745	13	891	2	972	13	3706	1	3821	12
90	20	341	5	563	8	746	12	892	2	973	13	3708	1	3822	12
91	19	347	1	564	8	747	7	893	2	975	14	3712	1	3823	13
92	20	349	1	580	11	754	15	894	2	976	14	3713	1	3824	13
93	19	350	1	581	11	758	15	895	9	977	14	3716	2	3825	14
94	20	351	1	597	7	760	1	898	16	986	9	3721	3	3826	14
95	19	352	1	598	7	761	1	899	2	987	9	3722	3	3827	14
99	19	353	1	600	4	762	18	900	13	988	9	3726	3	3828	12
101	20	355	15	601	4	772	9	902	3	989	9	3727	3	3829	12
102	19	356	15	602	4	775	6	904	10	991	8	3731	2	3830	15
103	19	367	9	603	4	776	2	905	10	992	8	3733	2	3831	2
104	20	368	9	604	4	778	3	906	10	993	8	3740	3	3832	2
105	20	369	9	605	4	780	12	907	10	995	6	3743	3	3833	2
106	20	370	11	606	13	781	12	909	9	996	6	3746	5	3834	3
107	19	371	11	608	13	782	12	910	9	3011	11	3747	5	3835	3
108	20	372	11	610	12	783	12	911	9	3012	11	3750	6	3836	3
111	20	400	14	611	12	791	5	912	9	3013	11	3752	6	3837	4
112	19	402	14	612	12	792	5	913	9	3021	17	3753	6	3838	5
113	19	407	15	613	12	793	5	915	4	3022	17	3755	6	3839	5
114	20	413	18	632	15	794	5	917	4	3023	17	3756	6	3840	5
115	19	414	18	640	17	796	5	918	14	3024	17	3760	7	3841	6
116	19	415	18	642	17	797	5	919	14	3031	16	3761	7	3842	7
121	19	420	12	644	17	798	5	920	14	3032	17	3765	7	3843	6
122	20	422	12	645	17	799	5	921	14	3033	17	3766	7	3844	6
123	20	433	16	646	17	800	5	922	14	3041	3	3768	8	3845	6
124	19	434	16	647	17	801	16	924	8	3042	3	3770	14	3846	6
125	20	435	16	648	17	806	7	926	8	3045	12	3772	15	3847	7
126	19	436	16	666	1	807	7	927	8	3046	12	3773	15	3848	7
208	4	437	16	676	12	809	5	928	8	3047	12	3774	15	3849	7
209	4	444	13	677	12	813	5	930	6	3051	10	3776	14	3850	8
210	4	445	13	680	12	814	1	931	6	3052	10	3777	15	3851	8
211	4	451	15	699	10	815	1	932	6	3053	10	3778	15	3852	12
221	3	452	15	700	10	816	1	934	10	3064	15	3779	15	3853	14
223	3	453	15	701	10	817	1	935	10	3072	17	3781	16	3854	14
224	3	469	10	702	10	818	2	936	10	3078	13	3782	17	3855	14
225	3	470	10	703	10	819	2	937	10	3325	6	3787	17	3856	14
300	14	471	10	704	10	820	5	938	16	3326	2	3790	16	3857	15
301	14	472	10	712	16	822	17	939	6	3328	1	3799	18	3858	15
304	1	498	1	718	4	823	6	943	8	3340	13	3801	1	3859	15
307	13	500	8	720	14	824	5	945	14	3341	13	3802	3	3860	15
309	2	501	8	721	14	825	5	946	13	3345	9	3803	3	3861	15
310	18	502	8	722	14	826	5	947	13	3346	9	3804	4	3862	16
311	6	503	8	725	13	827	5	948	15	3347	9	3805	4	3863	16
312	6	504	8	726	13	828	5	950	15	3348	9	3806	4	3864	16
315	3	517	7	727	13	829	11	951	14	3350	2	3807	5	3865	17
316	3	518	7	729	12	830	11	954	9	3354	2	3808	7	3866	17

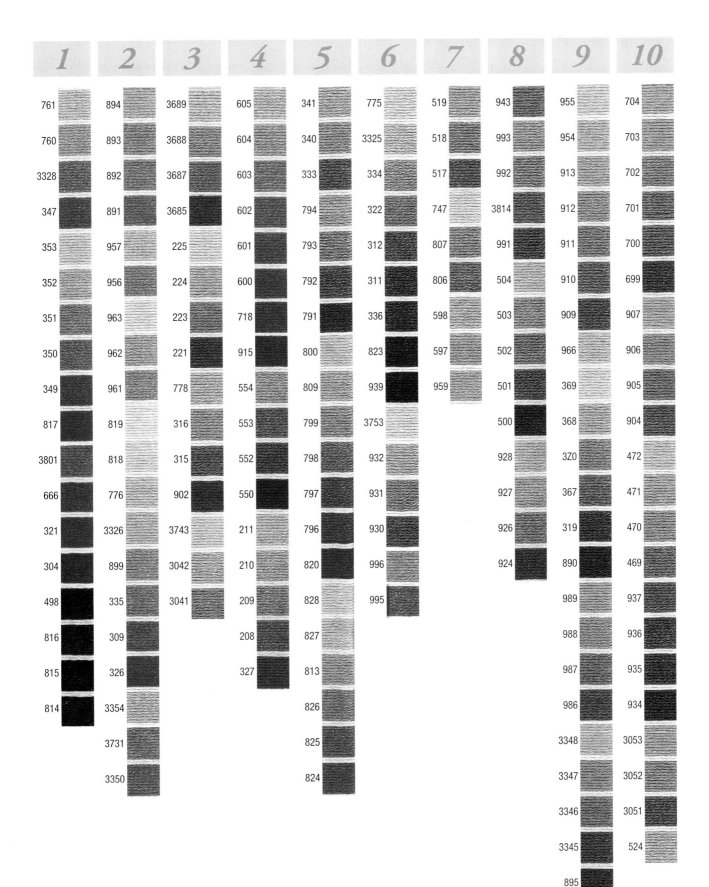

1
761
760
3328
347
353
352
351
350
349
817
3801
666
321
304
498
816
815
814

2
894
893
892
891
957
956
963
962
961
819
818
776
3326
899
335
309
326
3354
3731
3350

3
3689
3688
3687
3685
225
224
223
221
778
316
315
902
3743
3042
3041

4
605
604
603
602
601
600
718
915
554
553
552
550
211
210
209
208
327

5
341
340
333
794
793
792
791
800
809
799
798
797
796
820
828
827
813
826
825
824

6
775
3325
334
322
312
311
336
823
939
3753
932
931
930
996
995

7
519
518
517
747
807
806
598
597
959

8
943
993
992
3814
991
504
503
502
501
500
928
927
926
924

9
955
954
913
912
911
910
909
966
369
368
3Z0
367
319
890
989
988
987
986
3348
3347
3346
3345
895

10
704
703
702
701
700
699
907
906
905
904
472
471
470
469
937
936
935
934
3053
3052
3051
524

11	12	13	14	15	16	17	18	19	20
581	613	455	922	948	712	BS200	762	48	123
580	612	307	921	754	739	BLANC	415	116	125
734	611	444	920	758	738	ECRU	318	62	101
733	610	3078	919	356	437	822	414	112	114
732	3047	727	918	355	436	644	317	107	122
730	3046	726	951	950	435	642	413	57	92
3013	3045	725	945	407	434	640	310	75	94
3012	677	3823	402	632	433	3033		115	104
3011	422	745	301	453	801	3024		99	90
834	869	744	400	451	898	3022		95	108
832	420	743	300		938	3021		126	51
830	783	742	977		3371	3072		52	106
829	782	741	976		543	648		102	111
	781	740	975		842	647		93	61
	780	973			841	646		121	105
	746	972			840	645		67	69
	676	971			839	844		91	53
	729	947			838				
		946							
		900							
		608							
		606							

Suppliers

UK

Most large department stores carry a good range of fabrics, threads and accessories. Look in the Yellow Pages for details of your nearest haberdashers.

DMC Creative World Ltd
Head Office
Pullman Road
Wigston
Leicestershire
LE18 2DY
Tel: 0116 281 1040
DMC threads can be found in branches of Lewis's and Beatties nationwide. Phone for your nearest stockist.

Brett's Needlecraft Centre
4 College Street
Petersfield
GU32 4AD
Tel: 01730 266228

David Morgan Ltd
26 The Hayes
Cardiff
CF1 1UG
Tel: 029 2022 1011

Delicate Stitches
339 Kentish Town Road
London
NW5 2TJ
Tel: 020 7267 9403

The Embroidery Shop
51 William Street
Edinburgh EH3 7LW
Tel: 0131 225 8642
Fax: 0131 663 8255
Email: embroideryshop@gofornet.co.uk

Franklin & Sons
13a-15 St. Botolph's Street
Colchester
CO2 7DU
Tel: 01206 563955

Abakham Fabrics
111-115 Oldham Street
Manchester
M4 1LN
Tel: 0161 839 3229

Stitches
355 Warwick Road
Olton
Solihull
B91 1BQ
Tel: 0121 706 1048

Sussex Needlecraft
37 Warwick Street
Worthing
BN11 3DQ
Tel: 01903 823655

SOUTH AFRICA

The Cross Stitch Cottage
50 St Ledger Road
Claremont
Cape Town 7700
Tel: (021) 683 3279

Aladdins Cave
Shop 100
Kempton City
Kempton Park 1620
Tel: (011) 975 2116

Cross Stitch Connexion
Lifestyle Garden Centre
Cnr DF Malan & Ysterhoud
Randpark Ridge
Gauteng
Tel: (011) 793 2693

Needlewoman
Shop 44
Sanlam Plaza
Bloemfontein 9301
Tel: (051) 448 8151

The Image
8 LynnRidge Mall
Lynnwood Ridge
Pretoria 0082
Tel: (012) 361 1737

Thimbles & Threads
6 Quarry Centre
Hilton
Pietermaritzburg 3200
Tel: (033) 343 1966

AUSTRALIA

Barbour Threads Pty Ltd
Suite E3
2 Cowpasture Place
Wetherill Park
NSW 2164
Tel: (02) 9756 5466
Freecall: 1800 337 929

Birch Haberdashery and Craft
EC Birch Pty Ltd
Richmond
Victoria 3121
Tel: (03) 9429 4944

DMC Needlecraft Pty Ltd
51-55 Carrington Road
Marrickville
NSW 2204
Tel: (02) 9559 3088

Lincraft
Gallery level
Imperial Arcade
Pitt Street
Sydney
NSW 2000
Tel: (02) 9221 5111
(Stores nationwide)

Sewing Thread Specialists
41-43 Day Street (North)
Silverwater
NSW 2128
Tel: 1300 65 3855

Sullivans Haberdashery and Craft
Wholesalers
40 Parramatta Road
Underwood
Queensland 4119
Tel: (07) 3209 4799

NEW ZEALAND

The Embroiderer
140 Hinemoa Stree
Birkenhead
Auckland
Tel: (09) 419 0900

Nancy's Embroidery
273 Tinakori Road
Thorndon
Wellington
Tel: (04) 473 4047

Pauline's Needlecraft
94 Clyde Road
Browns Bay
Auckland
Tel: (09) 479 7783

Spotlight Stores
Carry a very large range of fabrics and
haberdashery materials
Manukau – Tel: (09) 263 6760
or 0800 162 373
Wairau Park – Tel: (09) 444 0220
or 0800 224 123
Hamilton – Tel: (07) 839 1793
New Plymouth – Tel: (06) 757 3575
Wellington – Tel: (04) 472 5600
Christchurch – Tel: (03) 377 6121

Stitches
351 Colombo Street
Sydenham
Christchurch
Tel: (03) 379 1868
Email: stitches@xtra.co.nz

For a wider listing of embroidery
suppliers nationwide, consult your
Yellow Pages under 'Handcrafts &
Supplies' or search under 'Shopping:
Hobbies & Games: Handcrafts' on
www.yellowpages.co.nz

Index